Magic in the Mountains

A Christmas Adventure

T. E. Milburn

To Bean and Gupkin,

for all the magic - for all the adventures!

TABLE OF CONTENTS

PROLOGUE

It was cold and dark in the cell where the captive was being held. He didn't know how long he'd been there, but he was keenly aware that he had been cut off completely from his magic. His red coat was torn and dirty, but he pulled it closely around him to stave off the chill that had seeped into his bones.

He heard the heavy thumping of boots above him, then the whining of the massive door as it was slowly pushed open. He knew the sound well—it was he who had overseen the construction of the solid wood door that guarded the dungeons below. He had also been the one to enchant the doorway so that no magic could be used beyond its opening.

Why had he insisted on making this prison? Others laughed and said it was a waste of time. There had never been a need for a jail in these parts, and there never would be. If only he had listened, he wouldn't be trapped down here, completely defenseless without his powers.

He took small comfort in knowing that he had been right about the need for a dungeon. For the past few years, something had been nagging at him, an inner voice that whispered that something was not quite right. While he didn't know who had planned the attack that led to his imprisonment, or why they had done it, he knew with sickening clarity that there was a dark force at work in his beloved land.

As the door opened, a bright light flooded the dungeon but was quickly blocked by a large figure whose face was hidden in shadow.

The figure slowly descended the stairs as the prisoner struggled to adjust his eyes to the light, but the captive didn't need to see the man's face to know who it was. He was the only other man in the North Pole.

"Hello Nick," the man said with an evil smile. "I trust you're enjoying the dungeons you so foolishly decided to build."

"Brother, what have you done?" Santa Claus said with despair as he hung his head and wept at a betrayal he never could have imagined.

A SLEEPY CRYSTAL

"This is going to be so epic," Alex James said as he excitedly shoved comic books into his empty suitcase.

"Those comic books aren't going to keep you very warm," his younger brother, Noah, said with a laugh. Noah carefully folded his own warmest clothes and placed them gently in his suitcase. "Mom says she's not packing for us this trip, so you better make sure you've got everything you need. I'm not leaving the mountain early just because you get cold and whiny. I plan on shredding all day every day."

"Don't worry about me, little bro," Alex said. "I can handle anything you can, and I don't need a hundred pairs of socks to outlast you on slopes. Besides, Mom and Dad said we are finally old enough to explore the mountain a bit on our own this trip, and I plan on seeing it all!"

"Just don't forget your snowboard . . . again," Noah teased.

"That was one time," Alex said with a smile. "I knew Mom and Dad would grab it. Besides, I'm ten now and clearly way more mature."

"Says the guy who just filled his suitcase with comic books . . . yeah, real mature," Noah joked.

Noah, who was only eight years old, often seemed the more grown-up of the two James brothers. While the brothers looked very similar with sandy brown hair and light blue eyes, the two could not be more different in personality.

Their half-full suitcases were perfect examples of just how different the two brothers were. While Alex randomly threw in whatever he felt like, Noah had made a list weeks ago so he wouldn't miss a thing.

Noah worked steadily through his list, checking off each item as it was packed until he had only one last thing to put in . . . his lucky crystal. He didn't leave home without it.

Two years before, on a family trip to Yellowstone National Park, he had found the crystal on the shore of the Firehole River while he and his brother were learning to fly-fish.

Alex was a natural and picked up fly-fishing with ease, even though he was only eight years old at the time. His parents had been so proud; they were always proud of Alex. To be fair, they were always proud of Noah too, but sometimes Noah wished things came to him as easily as they did his brother.

Noah had struggled to get the hang of fly-fishing and eventually lost interest, turning his attention instead to searching for treasures in the water. He had been wading through the shallows of the river when he spotted something that shined as brightly as a flashlight underwater. The light seemed to pulse as he moved closer. The nearer he got, the faster the light pulsed, like a quickening heartbeat. He finally closed his fingers around it and pulled the glowing object from the riverbed.

He peered into his hand to see a large crystal shining with an otherworldly glow. It emitted one final bright pulse, and then the light went out completely, leaving Noah holding what looked like a perfectly ordinary crystal. He moved it around, trying to get it to shine again, but it was as if it had suddenly gone to sleep. He shook his head, wondering if he had imagined what he had seen. Before he could investigate any further, he was interrupted by his family's cheers nearby.

Noah looked back up the river to see his mom with a large trout on her line. His dad and brother were crowded around her, examining the huge fish. They all looked so happy and excited, and even though he knew he was being silly, Noah couldn't help but feel a little bit excluded.

As he walked back up the river toward his parents and brother, he slipped the crystal into his pocket. His first instinct had been to rush over and share his find with his family, but ultimately, he decided to keep the treasure all to himself. He wasn't sure why, but he had the feeling that the crystal was meant to be his, that the glow had been a beacon calling him to it. But of course, he couldn't tell that to anyone else without sounding crazy. So, he decided to keep it a secret. For the past two years, he had managed to keep it hidden from his family.

Noah waited until Alex wasn't looking, then carefully placed the crystal inside his backpack. He checked it off his list right as his mom called him and Alex for dinner.

Noah turned and ran from his room because it was pizza night at the Jameses' house, and whoever was at the table first got to pick the best slices. He left his backpack on the bed so quickly he didn't even notice the entire thing had started to glow from within. After two years, the crystal was awake!

ROAD TRIP TO NOWHERE

The next morning, Alex and Noah were woken well before dawn by their parents, Anna and Edward James. Their parents always wanted to get on the road early when they went on family trips, thinking the boys would fall back to sleep as soon as they got in the car. Instead, both brothers were always too full of excitement to go back to sleep, and that morning was no different.

Every year since the boys were old enough to strap on a snowboard, the James family had spent two weeks during Christmas break at Whistler Blackcomb Ski Resort in Canada. The resort was about a nine-hour drive from their home in Post Falls, Idaho, and the trip to Canada always seemed like such a huge adventure.

Alex and Noah couldn't wait for the trip this year. Their parents had told them that they were finally old enough to check out the mountains on their own if they promised to always stick together and keep their walkie-talkies handy. Each member of the James family carried a small walkie-talkie on trips, as they often ventured to areas where cell phones didn't work.

The boys had complained about having to carry them until one day, Alex got separated from the group on a backcountry hike. He had panicked when he realized he was completely lost. But it was only moments before he found his family again, thanks to the walkie-talkie.

Unable to go back to sleep this particular morning, the boys sat in the back whispering about all the daring things they were going to try during their first solo outing. They liked snowboarding with their mom and dad, but the idea of freedom on the mountain to go wherever they wanted was just too exciting.

"Well, it's obvious you guys aren't sleepy. Who wants some powdered donuts and milk?" Anna asked while pulling out a surprise breakfast.

The sun was just starting to rise as they happily munched on their treats, daydreaming of all the fun . . . and all the snow.

"I can't wait to see how much powder they've got this year," Alex said between mouthfuls of donut. "I hope it's better than last year." It had been unseasonably warm then, and the snow had been a bit disappointing.

"If there's half as much powder as you've got all over your mouth, we're all set," Noah joked.

"Speaking of snow . . . incoming!" Edward said excitedly as he pointed to the flurries just beginning in the rosy morning dawn. "Looks like we won't have an issue with snow this year, boys."

But Mr. James was very wrong. The snow continued to pick up as the family drove north, making it more and more difficult to see. The snowstorm was whipping about with gathering force.

"This is taking forever," Noah whined as traffic slowed to a crawl.

"We're almost to the Canadian border," his mom said cheerfully. "Hopefully the storm will let up soon." She turned and smiled at the boys, but when she turned back to the front, Noah could see a worried look cross her face.

Half an hour later, Edward was pulling their SUV up to the Canadian border checkpoint. He handed the officer the family's passports and answered a few questions about where they were going and what they planned to do in the country.

"Be safe," the officer said as he cleared them for entry. "You guys are lucky, eh? If the storm keeps up like this, we're going to have to close the border until it clears up. I know you guys are trying to get to Whistler, but you might think about stopping someplace warm to wait out this blizzard."

"Thank you, Officer," Anna said.

"And Merry Christmas," Edward called out as he rolled his window back up and drove off again into the frosty morning.

"Maybe we should take his advice," Anna said quietly. "It really is getting risky out here."

"We're fine," replied Edward, but Noah noticed he was gripping the steering wheel so hard his knuckles were white. "We'll just keep it slow and steady, and we'll be there in no time."

But Mr. James was wrong for a second time that day. About forty miles farther down the highway, the family came to a road closure. All vehicles were forced to turn around due to hazardous conditions. They were told the storm was only going to intensify, and it was unlikely the road would be open for at least a day.

"Ahhh man, what are we going to do now?" Alex complained. "I don't want to go home!"

"No one is going home," his mother said. "I think I saw some hotels not too far back. Hopefully one has an open room and we can stop for just a night. Let's remember the rule about complaining on trips. Life will always throw curveballs, especially when you travel. You must be ready to roll with it; otherwise, you might miss out on some great adventures. I know this isn't ideal, but we'll make the most of it. Who knows, maybe we'll just manage to find some excitement."

"Excitement in the middle of nowhere, yeah right," Alex said under his breath as he rolled his eyes dramatically.

"I saw that," his mother said, but her attention was quickly diverted to a sign up ahead.

"North Point Ski Resort," Noah read aloud as they got closer.

"That's weird," said Edward. "In all of our times coming to Whistler, I've never seen that resort."

"Maybe it's new," Anna replied. "But the timing couldn't be better. I'm afraid we won't be able to see the highway at all if this snow continues. Let's check it out. It'll only be one night."

Edward took the exit, following the signs for the North Point Ski Resort. Ahead of them stood a very tall mountain with a long snow-covered road snaking its way up the side.

The family soon realized that theirs was the only car on the road as they slowly drove up the very steep incline. "Are you sure this is the right way?" Edward asked as their vehicle crept up the mountain.

Anna pulled out her phone to look for directions. "Hmmm, this place must be really new. There's no mention of it anywhere on Google. And the strangest thing is I can't even find this road on Google Maps . . . it's almost like it doesn't exist." Anna chuckled uneasily just as she looked down and realized she had lost service completely.

"Ha," Noah laughed, "it's like we've taken a road trip to nowhere."

"Dude, that sounds more like a Halloween-type adventure than a Christmas trip," Alex said.

"I don't know," Edward said, interrupting the boys' laughter. "Maybe we should just turn back. It's starting to get dark, and I can't see more than a few feet in front of me. We're not even sure there's a resort up here."

"Look! Up there." Noah pointed as a brightly lit building peeked out just beyond the next turn. "That's gotta be it," he continued excitedly.

Sure enough, they pulled into the empty parking lot for the North Point Ski Resort a moment later. "Where are all the cars?" Alex asked.

"I'm not sure, buddy," his father responded, then let out a little whistle. "Whew, I wonder how much this is going to cost."

Edward looked at the gorgeous building that stood before them. The resort was huge and shimmered like dark ice against the snowy mountain backdrop. The smoothness of the building was contrasted by an enormous amount of colorful stained glass. Every window and door had been intricately painted with beautiful patterns that made one think of Christmas. The effect was beyond magical!

"I love it," Anna exclaimed. "It's perfect, and we don't really have another choice. Let's just see if they're even open yet and if they have any rooms."

The family grabbed their luggage and left the car just as the storm hit a new level. They could barely see in front of them as they huddled together, walking as quickly as they could through the blizzard.

They had almost reached the doors when Noah suddenly had the most peculiar feeling that he was being watched. He looked around but could see nothing through the snowfall. He pulled his coat a bit tighter around his body and quickened his step.

BE OUR GUEST

The doors to the hotel opened before the family even reached them, held ajar by the most wonderful-looking character. The very small man at the entrance was dressed in long, thick robes made of rich velvet and silk fabrics. He had long silver hair and a matching beard, but the most noteworthy features of the strange man were his sharply pointed ears.

They guessed he was meant to be an elf because the ears were so distinctive. "How fun," whispered Anna. "It looks as if they are doing a Christmas theme at the hotel."

"Greetings, my friends," the man said in a voice that was deep and smooth. "I am Neethermire. I am in charge here, and you, dear family, are most welcome guests." Even though Neethermire was very small in stature, there was something very powerful about the man dressed as an elf.

"Oh, thank goodness you are open," Anna said as she brushed snow from herself before going too far into the lobby. "Do you have any rooms available for the night?"

"Indeed we do," responded Neethermire kindly. "But first, let's get you warmed up, shall we?" He led them into a grand lobby with rich wood floors the color of dark chocolate and walls the color of creamy eggnog.

"Wow!" Noah said, looking up to see golden ribbons that flowed across the soaring ceilings. Miniature hot air balloons the colors of rubies and emeralds drifted between them, held afloat by tiny flames that made the balloons glow. "This place is awesome," Noah said as he looked around in wonder.

At the center of the huge round room, a giant Christmas tree glistened with dazzling lights. It was beautifully decorated with sparkling balls, velvet bows, and the most amazing handcrafted ornaments. Tucked into the branches were freshly cut flowers, gold-flecked pinecones, and small bundles of cinnamon sticks that made the whole room smell of Christmas.

Neethermire led the family to an enormous stone fireplace that was blazing so hot they could feel the warmth from a few feet away.

Decorating the mantle of the fireplace was a collection of gorgeous snow globes, each with a different detailed scene. "Look at that one," Alex said. "Is that Santa's workshop? Wow, look at that. If you look closely enough, it's like you can almost see elves working inside."

"Whoa, check those out!" Noah said, turning his attention to two huge nutcrackers that stood guard on either side of the fireplace.

"Those are bigger than Dad," Alex said. "They look like they could do some serious damage in a fight."

"They've got nothing on me," Noah said, throwing a fake kick at his brother. Alex pretended to block Noah's kick and then threw a jab of his own.

Noticing a jar of giant candy canes on a nearby table, Alex grabbed one that was at least two feet long and pointed it at Noah like a sword. "On guard," Alex said.

Noah responded by grabbing his own candy cane and crouching into a dueling position. The two boys took turns thrusting and dodging each other's blows until Alex accidentally landed a hard strike on Noah's wrist.

"Ouch!" Noah cried. "That really hurt."

Before Alex had a chance to apologize, Neethermire interrupted. "Let's just get you checked in and save the combat for later, shall we?" Neethermire winked at Alex.

Feeling a little embarrassed, the boys quickly put down their candy cane swords.

Neethermire clapped his hands, and from seemingly nowhere, two more small people arrived. They were also dressed in beautiful robes and had sharply pointed ears. They held silver trays filled with steaming hot cocoa, pillowy whipped cream, and fluffy marshmallows that looked as if they had been slightly toasted over a fire. The elves began to sing as they offered the sweet drinks to the family. Their crystal-clear voices had a slight tinkling sound that reminded Noah of a wind chime.

"We've got a treat that can't be beat.
It's warm and yummy for your tummy.
Take a drink and you'll agree,
our cocoa is the best you'll see."

"Oh my gosh," Anna said after taking a sip. "This is truly the best hot cocoa I've ever had. What's your secret?"

"Oh, just a bit of magic," Neethermire said with a smile.

The family sipped their hot chocolates as they headed to the front desk to check in. The boys continued to wander around as their parents talked with Neethermire about the hotel. Noah was busy examining decorations on the massive Christmas tree when Alex suddenly grabbed his shoulder.

"Bro, you left your flashlight on again!" Alex said.

"What are you talking about?" Noah asked, until he looked down and saw his backpack aglow. "What the heck, I didn't even bring a flashlight," he said loudly, just as the light went out again.

"Everything good, boys?" Edward asked as he and Anna finished up. "Who wants to check out the indoor water park?"

"Water park, no way!" the boys exclaimed at the same time. "Let's go," they said, forgetting all about the shining backpack.

They were so excited they never even noticed the girl with glittering green eyes watching them intently from the shadows.

WATERPARK OF WONDERS

The family followed one of the staff as they were led to their room. Along the way, they passed other employees all costumed similarly. "This is great," Noah said excitedly. "Are all the people who work here dressed as elves?"

"Why yes, they are indeed dressed like elves," their guide said with a little smile. "It's like it's their natural state." She chuckled slightly.

The James family continued to follow as the elf guide showed them the hotel. The inside truly was a wonder, as the Christmas theme continued throughout the entire place.

Anna was particularly impressed with the decorations and pulled out her camera to take pictures. She snapped a few photos of the hotel, then asked the boys to pose for her.

Noah and Alex grinned with silly smiles as they stood in front of what looked like an antique toy shop. Wooden rocking horses that moved on their own, porcelain dolls that seemed just on the verge of speaking, ornate toy soldiers, and cuddly teddy bears made up the background of the photo.

When Anna was done, she looked at their guide, who was staring intensely at her sons. Feeling uncomfortable, she put her camera away and asked that they go straight to the room.

"Don't you want to see the rest?" the elf asked hopefully. "We've worked so hard to make it perfect for you . . . for all our guests, of course."

"We'll see it all after a little time at the water park and some dinner," Anna said. "Thank you, but it's been a long day."

"As you wish," the woman replied with what seemed like a hint of disappointment.

They reached their room and the guide said goodbye, directing the family to the restaurant and the water park.

"Wow, what a place," Edward remarked as they closed the door and looked around their room. A fire was crackling merrily in the fireplace, and more hot cocoa had been left on a table between two cozy chairs in front of the fire. There was a small Christmas tree sparkling in the corner of the main room. The bedroom was separated by French doors and had two plush beds that the boys couldn't resist immediately jumping on.

"No jumping on the beds," Edward said half-heartedly. He remembered from his own childhood just how much fun it was to hop from bed to bed in a hotel room.

"Forget about the water park," Alex joked as he walked into the bathroom and saw a bathtub the size of a small pool. "I'm just gonna stay in the tub all night."

"Speaking of the water park, last one in their swim trunks is a one-eyed pig monster!" Noah yelled as he leapt for his suitcase.

"Wait, you brought swim trunks?" Alex asked, realizing he had forgotten to pack his own.

"Don't worry. I brought a pair just in case you forgot," Anna said as she pulled a pair of Alex's swim trunks from her bag with a wink.

"Thanks Mom." Alex grinned, giving her a huge hug.

"I win by default," Noah said, even though he hadn't found his swim shorts yet. "You're disqualified because you didn't pack your own."

"Am not! And it looks like you're the one-eyed pig monster," Alex said, laughing loudly as he pulled on his shorts. Noah found his trunks and put them on, making sure to slip his lucky crystal into a zippered pocket when no one was looking.

When everyone was ready, the family headed out to find the water park. As they walked down the empty halls, they realized they hadn't seen another guest since they arrived. "Maybe the weather is keeping everyone away," Edward guessed. "But I'm not complaining. It seems like we've got the whole place to ourselves."

The boys' jaws dropped when they finally got to the huge glass doors that separated the water park from the rest of the hotel. The Christmas theme continued through the magical water park, with colorful holiday decorations everywhere.

The waterslides were built into the sides of small snowcapped mountains, while hidden pools were carved into frozen caves. Beautiful ice sculptures of artic animals sparkled in the bright light. There was even a miniature version of the Polar Express train that circled around the park, dropping off rafts and pool toys as it went.

Noah noticed that there were large icicles hanging all over the ceiling. He expected it to be freezing inside, but the warm air that surrounded them as they walked through the doors was perfect.

They headed straight toward a slide called the Avalanche, where they each grabbed a raft and walked the steep hill to the top. Alex had called going first, but he hesitated once he saw the swirling waters at the entrance. Rather than being an open waterslide, the Avalanche traveled inside the mountain, and they could see no light coming from within.

"Guess they want you to experience what it's like being buried by an avalanche," Alex said, laughing nervously.

"You're just being a scaredy cat," Noah said and moved to be the first one in.

Edward could tell Noah was a little scared too, so he stepped in front of him. "Let me show you boys how it's done. Whoo-hoo!" he yelled as he flopped belly-first on his raft and headed down the slide.

It seemed to take forever, but they finally heard him yell "That was awesome!" as he splashed down in a pool far below.

Noah was nervous as he prepared for his turn. He tried to muster his dad's courage as he stared down the dark tunnel. "Whoo-hoo," he said softly as he jumped into the slide's opening.

Noah was frightened at first as he zoomed downward in the pitch black. However, after a few seconds, he could see a glow shining up ahead. Within no time, he was surrounded by bright, streaking lights. He imagined this was what flying through space at warp speed would look like as he whizzed through the slide.

"Whoooo!" Noah yelled. He was going so fast, but he was no longer afraid.

Then, suddenly, he stopped. He hadn't been spit out into the pool below, but was rather stuck somewhere in the middle of the slide. The water had dried up without warning. Fear crept along Noah's spine as he tried to figure out what had just happened.

He had decided that he would have to just scoot the rest of the way down the dry slide when suddenly, a man's deep voice boomed around him, echoing through the tunnel.

"If you are hearing this, it means that I was unable to fight off my attackers. I am leaving this message as dark forces bear down upon me. I do not know why they come or what they plan, but I know that I need your help, Sons of the Crystal. You must find me before it's too late. Bring your crystal—" The voice was cut off mid-sentence by what sounded like a loud crash. Then all went silent.

Before Noah could even think, the water suddenly returned and swept him down the slide. He had never been more relieved than when he splashed out into the deep pool at the bottom and saw his dad waiting for him.

"Pretty cool, huh?" Edward asked as Noah swam to the edge of the pool. "All those lights, all those sounds?"

"Ummm, it was pretty weird," Noah said, thinking his dad must've had the same experience. But before he could say any more, Alex was spit from the mouth of the slide.

"Let's do it again!" his brother yelled.

"I think I'm going to check out something else," Noah said. It might not have freaked his dad or brother out, but there was no way he was going back inside the Avalanche.

Noah's mom agreed to go explore with him, while his dad and Alex went back up the hill for another ride.

Noah and his mom went to ride some other fun slides. Next, they floated down a lazy river that was bordered on both sides by snowy banks scattered with pine trees. Then they headed to the wave pool, where they were shocked to see what looked like real penguins on snow-covered rocks behind the pool.

"Wow!" Anna said. "Those are so lifelike; they must've spent a fortune on this place."

Noah and Anna played in the waves for a while before finally being joined by Edward and Alex. "I'm starving," Alex said as he jumped a wave crashing toward him.

"What's new?" Anna asked, laughing.

"Alright, let's get some dinner, and then maybe a movie before bed. How does that sound?" Edward asked as they packed up to leave.

Noah was following his family out when he thought he saw something move out of the corner of his eye. He looked around him, but saw nothing. Still, he hurried his pace so he could walk right next to his dad. As fun as this water park had been, he had to admit it kind of gave him the creeps.

"That was too close," a small goblin-like creature snarled as he stepped from his hiding place. "We were almost seen."

"Yes, but we weren't," another creature said with a wicked smile. "All is still on track. Tomorrow, the boys will be ours, and then we will put an end to Christmas once and for all!"

5

MAGIC IN THE MOUNTAINS

Early the next morning, Noah bolted awake from a terrible dream. His hands were shaking and his heart was racing as he sat up in bed recalling the nightmares that troubled his sleep all night. All he could remember of his dreams was the feeling of being trapped somewhere dark, and no matter how hard he tried, he couldn't escape.

Rubbing his eyes, Noah quietly crept into bed with his parents. He let out a long sigh as he snuggled in between his mom and dad, and after a few moments, he fell back asleep.

A couple hours later, the whole family woke as the sun made its way into the sky. "Wow, these beds are amazing," Anna said as she hopped lightly from bed. "I can't remember when I've last had such a great night's sleep."

"Me too," said Edward. "I know I had the most wonderful dreams all night, but I can't seem to remember them now."

"Not me," groaned Noah. "I feel like I barely slept."

Before he could continue, his mom threw open the curtains, and bright morning light came blazing into the room. All attention was turned to the landscape just outside their balcony. The family had arrived the day before, after it was already dark, so they hadn't seen the view yet.

"Woah! Check that out!" Alex said as he looked outside at the perfect ski conditions. The sun sparkled on snow-covered mountains like millions of glittering diamonds. The runs were groomed, the chairlifts were empty, and best of all, there were inches of fresh powder that looked completely untouched by any other skier or snowboarder.

"Can we please stay here for the day?" Alex begged. "There's no one out there. Think of how awesome it would be."

Instantly forgetting his bad dreams at seeing such a winter wonderland, Noah joined his brother in convincing his parents to let them stay. "Please guys, we have to check this place out."

"Alright, alright, we'll see," Edward said cheerily, although neither he nor Anna needed much convincing to change up their plans. The slopes did indeed look amazing, and Whistler could wait.

The boys scrambled to get on their snow gear with the hope that their parents would agree to stay. Noah double-checked he had everything, then tripled-checked he had his lucky crystal.

They finished getting ready and then headed down for breakfast, where they found Neethermire waiting for them in the restaurant.

"Good morning, James family. Did you all have a restful night?" Neethermire asked, staring intensely at Noah.

Noah looked away, feeling a little uncomfortable with Neethermire's attention. He knew he was being silly, but it was as if the strange man knew all about Noah's bad dreams.

"I slept like a baby," Anna said with a smile. "This place is so quiet and peaceful."

"Speaking of quiet, it feels like we are the only guests here," Edward said questioningly.

"Yes, I'm afraid the weather has blocked all the highways, so you are the only people here," Neethermire replied. "In fact, it looks like it might be some time before the roads are open again."

"So, you're saying we couldn't leave even if we wanted to?" Alex asked hopefully.

"Quite right, dear boy. It looks as though you are trapped here with us," Neethermire said with a wink.

"Yes!" both Noah and Alex said, barely able to contain their excitement.

"Well, I will wish you a good day then. Be safe on the slopes, and most of all, have fun. I will have the chef prepare something special for dinner tonight once you have all worked up an appetite," Neethermire said as he walked away, suddenly seeming as if he was in a hurry.

"I hope it's pizza," whispered Alex to his brother as they sat down to breakfast. They chose a table near a large fireplace with flames crackling merrily in the hearth.

"You always hope it's pizza," Noah said with a laugh, just as three servers arrived with trays piled high with all kinds of breakfast foods. There were fluffy chocolate chip pancakes, golden waffles with an assortment of toppings, sweet French toast, cheesy omelets, crispy fried eggs, and a variety of ripe fruits. Best of all, though, was another tray of the hot cocoa they had enjoyed the night before.

After a wonderful breakfast, they headed out to the slopes, where their snowboards and helmets were all lined up, waiting for them.

Noah was the first to grab his gear. "Race you," he yelled to his brother as he hurried to the nearest chairlift. Alex and his parents were a minute behind him, so Noah studied the map of the ski runs as he waited for them to catch up.

"Whoa," he said to himself as he realized they would have the whole place to themselves. While he was really excited at the idea, he couldn't help but think it was strange that no one else was around. He reached into his pocket and rubbed his lucky crystal, which was his habit whenever he felt a little uneasy.

Alex and Noah were the first to get on the chairlift, their parents right behind them. As the lift took them smoothly up to the peak, Alex said, loudly enough for everyone to hear, "What's a snowman's favorite food?"

"I don't know, what?" Noah replied.

"A brrrr-ito," Alex said, cracking everybody up. Their laughter echoed off the surrounding mountains as they neared the top.

They spent the next few hours exploring North Point Mountain. They had the most amazing time racing down the slopes, practicing tricks in the terrain park, and playing in all the fresh powder.

"Alright boys," Anna said as they reached the bottom of a blue slope. "Your dad and I decided you can take a few runs on your own while we go back to those double black diamond trails we saw off chair six. Just meet us back here in an hour for lunch."

"Freedom!" Alex yelled as he pumped his fist in the air. "Let's head back to the terrain park. I want to hit up the half-pipe!"

Noah wasn't excited to be without his parents, but he didn't want his brother to think he was being a baby, so he followed him to the chairlift while his parents headed in a different direction.

"Make sure to keep your walkie-talkies on," Edward yelled from a distance.

The boys breathed in the cold winter air as they made their way back up the mountain in silence.

"You nervous?" Noah finally asked, noticing that Alex had gotten quiet as soon as their parents were out of sight.

"Nah, not really," Alex said, but Noah didn't believe him.

"Well, I kind of am," admitted Noah sheepishly. "I mean, we've never been by ourselves on a mountain before, and there's no one around if we come across any trouble."

"Stop worrying, we'll be fine," Alex said. "Besides, we've got our walkie-talkies, and Mom and Dad have theirs just in case."

They exited the chairlift when they got to the top, strapped into their snowboards, and headed straight to the terrain park. "I call first on the pipe," Alex shouted as he took off ahead of his brother, but when they got to the half-pipe, they were shocked to see someone already there.

A kid was absolutely shredding the half-pipe—doing tricks the brothers had only seen at competitions. The snowboarder was catching huge air while effortlessly doing backflips, alley-oops, and even a Double McTwist 1260, combining three-and-a-half twists and two flips in one piece of air.

The kid waved to the boys to drop in after coming to a stop at the end of the half-pipe. While neither Alex nor Noah had skills anywhere near what they had just watched, they charged ahead anyway.

Alex went first, displaying what few tricks he could do, like toe grabs, heel grabs, and even an attempt at a backside air.

Noah dropped in shortly after Alex, leaving plenty of room between them. He had been studying videos of professional snowboarders for months with the hope that he could learn some new skills. He carved cleanly through the pipe but wasn't quite ready for any big tricks.

When Noah came to the end, he heard his brother excitedly talking to the other kid. "This is my brother," Alex said as Noah came to a stop.

"Hey, I'm Noah," he said as he took off his goggles and helmet to introduce himself.

Noah and Alex were both shocked when the other kid took off her helmet and long, black, curly hair came spilling out. She pulled off her goggles, revealing bright green eyes that glittered like emeralds against her dark skin.

"You're a girl," Alex sputtered before he could stop himself. "Um, I mean of course you're a girl. It's just, I uh, thought you were a boy."

Noah could tell Alex was nervous. Lately whenever he was around girls, he always seemed a little funny. "What's your name?" Noah asked, saving his brother from further humiliation.

"I'm Izzy. Nice to meet you guys," she said, apparently unaware of Alex's awkwardness. "What are you guys doing out here? I thought I was the only one here."

"We were going to ask you the same thing. Neethermire told us there was no one else staying at the resort," Alex said, getting back his confidence.

"Oh, I live around here. I just hike in when I want a day on the slopes," Izzy said. "I know this mountain like the back of my hand. I can show you guys some secret spots with huge jumps if you'd like." She smiled shyly at Alex.

Noah hesitated, but before he could say no thank you, Alex replied, "That would be awesome!"

"Great, strap in and follow me," Izzy said. "You're going to see things you've never seen before; I promise you that."

"We really shouldn't," Noah whispered into his brother's ear. "We've got to be back to meet Mom and Dad in about forty minutes."

"It's fine," Alex said. He was ready to follow Izzy, who was already carving her way down the mountain. "We'll be back in time." And with that, he pointed his board downhill and took off after their new friend.

While he didn't think his brother would desert him on the mountain, Noah felt he had no choice but to follow.

Sure enough, Alex turned around a few seconds later to make sure his little brother was behind him. It reminded Noah that Alex was always looking out for him.

Izzy was true to her word as the boys followed her down some amazing unmarked trails. The three of them shredded the mountain for about thirty minutes before they stopped for a break. "We'd better head back," Alex said breathlessly.

"Just one more trail. It'll take us back down to the base anyway. I promise this one will be the best," Izzy said with a hopeful look.

"Alright, as long as it's quick," Alex said. "And maybe we can ride some more after lunch."

"Maybe," Izzy said distractedly as she scanned the tree line, searching intently. She spotted whatever she was looking for and headed out.

Noah assumed she was looking for another jump, but rather than following the trail, Izzy quickly turned and headed into the forest.

"You know we're not allowed to ride in the trees," Noah said anxiously as he realized Alex meant to follow Izzy.

"We don't even know where we are," Alex responded quickly, a hint of fear in his voice. "All of these trails are unmarked; I'm not sure we can even find our way back without her. C'mon, we've got to keep up." Alex took off after Izzy.

Noah truly had no choice this time, so he reluctantly followed his brother. Noah's heart raced as he dodged the trees all around, trying to catch up to Izzy, who maintained a dangerous speed.

Alex stayed close to Noah, and they soon lost sight of Izzy, only to spot her again not far ahead. She was heading straight toward an enormous tree.

"Watch out!" Alex screamed as she careened toward the giant pine, but just as she was about to smash into it, a bright circle of light surrounded her, and she disappeared into thin air.

Alex tried to stop himself, but he was going too fast. Noah watched helplessly as Alex put a protective arm in front of his face, trying to shield himself from the unknown, but within seconds the light overtook him too. He was gone!

Panic gripped Noah as he continued to race forward. There was no stopping. He closed his eyes and waited for the light.

SONS OF THE CRYSTAL

Blazing brightness surrounded Noah as momentum carried him forward. He struggled to stay upright on his snowboard as he slid through a tunnel of light.

Then, just as quickly as the light had appeared, it was gone, leaving Noah snowboarding through a forest that looked completely different from the place they had just been.

He spotted Alex just ahead and skidded to a stop next to his brother, who was bent over like he was going to be sick.

"Are you OK?" Noah asked, shaking with fear.

"I think I'm OK, just totally freaked out," Alex said as the boys unstrapped their snowboards and looked around. "What the heck was that? And where the heck are we?"

The forest now surrounding them was a stark contrast to where they had just been. While the weather at North Point

Mountain had been sunny and clear, wherever they were now was dull, gray, and lifeless. The boys were still surrounded by pines, but these ones seemed to be dying, as they were all beginning to turn brown and drop their needles. The trees were adorned with what looked like Christmas decorations. However, these ornaments looked drab and colorless, as if the joy had been sucked right out of them.

Even the snow beneath them looked different. It still sparkled like tiny diamonds, but rather than looking pure and white, it took on a purplish hue, as if someone was shining a black light on it.

A chill ran up Noah's spine as he realized that wherever they were was far away from North Point Mountain.

"Look, up there!" Noah said. "In that clearing, I think that's Izzy."

Sure enough, the boys could see Izzy about fifty feet ahead of them at the edge of an open field. As Alex and Noah approached, they could see she was looking nervously all around her. She jumped like a scared rabbit when Noah called her name.

"Oh, hey guys," Izzy said uneasily.

"What is going on here? Where are we?" Alex demanded. "All I know is that we were following you, and then all of a sudden, boom, we're in this wasteland."

"You were wrong to trust me," Izzy said sadly. "I know you'll never forgive me, but I didn't have a choice." She looked as if she was going to cry. "It doesn't matter now. They will be here any moment."

"Who will be here?" Noah asked, feeling sorry for Izzy. She seemed so miserable.

Then suddenly, a sound of bells dinged in the distance. A second later, the boys saw movement at the other end of the field. They watched nervously as snow was whipped up on the horizon. Three fast-approaching sleighs were headed straight toward them, pulled by teams of reindeer. Sitting atop the sleighs, whipping the reindeer to go faster, were small knobby-looking creatures.

About four feet tall, the little beings resembled goblins the boys had seen in storybooks. With wrinkled green skin, small squinty eyes, large noses, and sharply pointed ears, the creatures coming toward them looked both fierce and determined.

The chiming of the bells grew louder and louder as Alex and Noah stared in disbelief at the sleighs drawing closer. They reached out and took each other's hand, a shared feeling of dread passing between them. Noah shoved his other hand into the pocket of his snowboard pants so that he could grip his lucky crystal.

Hoping it would give him some courage, he pulled the crystal from his pocket. He looked down, only to be stunned when a light shot from the point of the crystal, stretching out at least a hundred feet in the air.

Noah turned to see Alex and Izzy both staring in amazement.

"What is happening? How are you doing that?" Alex asked, but Izzy interrupted him.

"Oh no! What have I done?" she said, her voice trembling. "They told me they would let my parents go if I brought them the two human boys. I had no idea that you are the Sons of the Crystal—and I have delivered you to the enemy."

"What are you saying?" Alex tried to ask, but Izzy cut him off.

"You must go! Now!" Izzy screamed wildly.

"But where are we supposed to go? I don't even know where we are," Noah said.

"Use the crystal! It has a strong magic that will allow you to open a portal like the one we came through. If the legends are correct, either one of you should be able to use it," Izzy said. "Just hold it, picture where you want to go, and it will take you there. But go now!"

"Come with us!" Noah said, as he could see the sleighs closing in on them.

Izzy shook her head. "I can't go. My family will suffer more than they already have. Just go!"

"We have to get out of here," Alex said frantically. "I don't want to find out what those things want with us."

Knowing his brother was right, and also realizing there was no convincing Izzy to join them, Noah grasped the crystal tightly with both hands. He didn't necessarily believe this crystal would magically transport them, but then again, he had seen a lot of things in the past few minutes that defied belief.

"Here goes nothing," he said, the sleighs almost upon them. He closed his eyes and envisioned where he wanted to go. A bright portal opened about twenty feet behind them. The boys picked up their snowboards and ran as quickly as they could toward the light until they seemed to be inside it, but nothing happened.

Noah turned around to look at Izzy one last time. She was on her knees, surrounded by several of the small goblins that had jumped from the sleighs. Her head hung down so that Noah couldn't see her face, but he could tell by the shaking of her shoulders that she was crying.

The other creatures raced toward the boys wielding long hammer-like weapons. One goblin, almost in striking distance, raised his weapon. The boys instinctively raised their arms for protection and closed their eyes against the attack. When no blow was landed, they opened their eyes and realized they were once again surrounded by a tunnel of light. The next thing they knew, they were back in the forest on North Point Mountain.

"Really?" Alex asked. "Izzy said picture anywhere you want to go, and you brought us back here? You could have envisioned the hotel, and we could be with Mom and Dad right now. Instead, I'm not even sure we can find our way back from here."

"Give me a break," Noah said angrily. "It's not like I have experience with magic crystals. It was the first place I thought of. If you're such an expert, why don't you use it and get us back to the hotel?"

"I would, but I don't want anything else to do with whatever those portals are," Alex said. "And where did you get that thing anyway?" He gestured toward the crystal that Noah still held firmly.

Noah told his brother the story of how he had found the crystal years before in the river and had decided to keep it a secret.

"Really bro, you found a glowing crystal and you didn't think you should tell me," Alex said. He looked hurt that his brother would keep such a big secret from him when they told each other everything.

"I don't know," Noah said as he looked down at his feet. "I guess I thought maybe you guys wouldn't have believed me. Anyway, I should have told you."

"Yeah, well whatever," Alex said. "Let's just strap on our boards and find our way down the mountain."

Alex started off, with Noah following right behind him. They picked a trail and went as fast as they could, praying that nothing had followed them through the tunnel of light.

It turned out that the trail they chose linked back up with one of the main runs on the mountain, and they could see the resort ahead of them in no time. The golden, warm lights of the hotel offered some comfort before they even reached the bottom. They knew their parents would be waiting for them, and that they'd probably be very worried because the boys were late for their meet-up.

As they got closer to the bottom, the boys scanned the area for their mom and dad, but couldn't see them anywhere. They tried their walkie-talkies, but got no answer from their parents.

"Where are they?" Noah said, but just then he saw Neethermire running from the hotel with a very worried look on his face.

"What's wrong?" Alex asked as they stopped in front of the hotel manager. "Where are our parents? They were supposed to meet us here."

"Your parents have been taken," Neethermire said without emotion. "Come quickly, we have much to talk about."

CHRISTMAS MAGIC

"Taken? What do you mean?" Alex demanded. "I'm not going anywhere without seeing my parents."

"I will explain everything, but you must trust me and follow me now. I misjudged our enemy. I didn't think they could travel the portals, but I was wrong, and now they are among us. You should be safe inside, where the magic is still strong."

Alex and Noah shared a worried look. "How do we know we can trust him?" Noah whispered to his brother. "You insisted that we follow Izzy and look where that got us."

"I don't see any other options," Alex said, ignoring Noah's accusation. "Mom and Dad must be in some kind of trouble or they would have been waiting for us. We're in the middle of nowhere, with no way to get help. Just keep that crystal ready in case we need a quick getaway."

The boys followed Neethermire inside the hotel. He led them to the giant fireplace, where he had hot cocoa waiting for them. "Drink, boys. It will help warm you up."

"I don't want any hot chocolate," Noah said, still shaking with fear. "I want my parents. Where are they?"

"Very well," Neethermire said. "I will tell you what I can. Your parents have been kidnapped by a dark force. This enemy seeks to destroy Christmas and all the magic that goes along with it. If they succeed, the world as you know it will be changed forever."

"Christmas? What are you even talking about? What does any of this have to do with Christmas?" Alex asked.

Neethermire paused for a moment, gathering his thoughts. "Have you not guessed it yet? Well, first let me introduce myself properly. I am Neethermire Oloren, the oldest living elf in the world and the chief assistant to Santa Claus. At least I was until three weeks ago, when Santa's brother, Malachi, organized a plot to take over Christmas. Malachi and his allies imprisoned Santa in the dungeons of the North Pole, stealing his crystal and cutting him off from his magic."

"Wait, so you're saying that you're a real elf . . . not just wearing a costume?" Noah asked skeptically. "And let me get this straight, you're also saying that Santa Claus is real?"

"Why of course he is real. And so is Christmas magic. People feel a mysterious happiness as Christmas draws close each year. They seek out those they love and slow their lives to enjoy the things that really matter. They bask in the warmth of family and friendship, and remember how simple joy can be. This, my friends, is Christmas magic, an ancient force that brings people together.

"But the magic of Christmas is actually a cycle," Neethermire continued. "Christmas magic brings people together, but the joy they experience during the season then flows back to the North Pole, where it becomes Christmas magic. It is stored in a secret location until the following Christmas, when it is automatically released as the holiday season draws close.

"If Malachi and his gang have their way, that magic will be snuffed out like a candle. Just one Christmas missed could break the cycle, and I fear the results would be devastating," Neethermire explained. "The wonder and happiness that come each December would be no more, and without it, friends will lose touch, families will stray farther apart, and that lack of togetherness will have echoing consequences throughout the year. Life will be gray without the bonds of love and companionship that are strengthened each holiday season."

"Like actually gray?" Alex interrupted. "Wherever we were today seemed pretty depressing. Everything just seemed dark and gloomy."

"I was just coming to that. My elves gave me full reports on everything that happened," Neethermire said. "You boys visited the North Pole today. The darkness you saw there is the result of Santa being cut off from Christmas magic. The North Pole is dying without him. While the magic does not belong to Santa, he is the only one that can wield it."

"OK, but how did we even get there?" Alex asked, beginning to accept the things he was hearing.

"You were taken by way of a portal that can only be accessed by elves or Santa himself. There are portals all over Earth that allow us to travel between the North Pole and your world. We know that it was Izzy who led you through."

"Wait, Izzy is an elf?" Noah asked with disbelief.

"Yes, Izzy is still a very young elf, and her features have not fully developed. As she grows, she will start to look more like the other elves you have seen around the hotel," Neethermire explained. "I am Izzy's uncle. She fled here with me when her parents were taken captive. Many of Santa's closest friends were rounded up and thrown in the dungeons with him." Neethermire shook his head sadly.

"Izzy is as pure of heart as any elf I've ever known, so I know she felt she had no choice but to betray you. What I don't know is how the enemy was able to reach Izzy in order to force her to help them. She should have been safe here," Neethermire said.

As if in answer to his question, a group of strong-looking elves marched into the lobby, wearing swords at their hips like soldiers. They were forcefully leading two of the strange little creatures the boys had seen in the woods earlier.

"Let us go!" one of the goblins hissed. "You've got no cause to hold us."

Neethermire stood, drawing himself up to his full height. Even though he was quite small by human standards, he towered over the goblins. His rich voice boomed as he spoke. "You violate the ancient laws by even being in this realm. Your race was banished from both the North Pole and the human world long ago, after you unsuccessfully grabbed for a power that was not yours."

"Yes, but we won't be unsuccessful this time," the bolder of the two creatures said with an oily grin. "That niece of yours might have screwed things up temporarily, but not to worry, the boys will be ours soon. You think all elves are loyal to your precious Santa Claus, but there are those among your kind who also seek his ruin. How do you think we got their parents?"

Alex lunged at the goblin, but Neethermire quickly blocked him from grabbing the creature. "Do not get too close," he warned. "They are a vile species, and their bite is poisonous to humans."

"But he just said he knows what happened to our parents," Alex fired back. "They have to tell us where they are!"

"Oh, I'll tell you where they are," the goblin said with a wicked sneer. "By now they should be locked up right next to Santa, just waiting for you boys to come and save them. But not to worry, they are safe . . . for now."

"Enough!" Neethermire commanded. "Get them out of my sight. Lock them in the cellars until we figure out the proper punishment." He said the last words slowly, fixing his gaze upon the goblins.

As the elves led the goblins away roughly, one continued to yell. "Tick tock, boys! You'd better get going if you want to reach your parents in time. Malachi is not known to be patient."

"Come on, we've got to go," Noah said once the goblins were gone. "You heard them, we've got to go get Mom and Dad!"

"Slow yourself, child," Neethermire said. "You boys are clearly very brave, but there are still many things you must know if we stand any chance of getting your parents back."

"You can tell us on the way," Alex said, "but we're going to get our parents."

Just then, loud shouting and the clanging of metal erupted down one of the halls. The noises grew closer, and in seconds, the boys could see that the group of soldier elves was locked in battle with a small army of goblins.

The goblins had maces, clubs, and large war hammers. They were effectively pushing the elves back into the main lobby, where the boys and Neethermire stood near the fire.

It was clear the elves were skilled swordsmen as they fought furiously against the enemy. They parried the attacks of the small creatures, holding them at bay as long as they could, but the sheer number of the goblins was beginning to overwhelm the elf forces.

"Get the boys!" the oily goblin from before screeched. Having escaped from his captors, he appeared to be the leader. At his direction, the rest of the goblin force let out a wild cry and intensified their efforts.

Neethermire did not panic, but rather turned to the boys and said calmly, "There is no more time. You must go now. I didn't want to believe it, but these goblins could only have breached the magical seal of this hotel with help from elves. This place is meant to be a haven, but clearly it is no longer safe."

"Then let's go!" Alex yelled above the crashing sounds of battle. He began to run for the doors, but Neethermire stopped him.

"You must use the crystal's magic and go back to the North Pole. We elves must use the existing portals, but the crystal will allow you to open a new portal and transport yourself from anywhere," Neethermire said. He pulled one of the snow globes the boys had admired earlier from the mantle of the fireplace. The specific globe he chose had a small but cheery-looking cabin inside. It sat on a frozen lake, surrounded by trees. "Here, use this as a guide. Think of the North Pole, and then picture this cabin. It will take you to friends. They will help you decide what to do next. Now go!"

"Wait, you're not coming?" Noah asked worriedly.

"I will follow when I can, but there are things here I must attend to first," Neethermire said, a sense of urgency creeping into his voice. Again, he told the boys to go, but this time he left no room for questioning.

While the elves were still managing to hold the snarling creatures back, the goblins were slowly gaining ground and closing in on the boys. Noah pulled the crystal from his pocket and focused on the scene inside the snow globe, willing himself to go there. Like before, a gateway of light opened nearby, and the boys ran for it.

The goblins howled as they saw the boys heading for the portal. "Stop them!" the leader screamed, but it was too late. The last thing the boys saw before the light closed around them was Neethermire touching the giant nutcrackers that were on the sides of the fireplace. The nutcrackers came to life instantly, and followed Neethermire as he rushed into the fray.

A CABIN IN THE WOODS

While the boys were kind of getting the hang of traveling by portals after three trips, both Noah and Alex were full of dread as they emerged from the light. They didn't know what they would find on the other side. Would they have even traveled to the right spot, and would there be friends as Neethermire had said? Or would there be more of those gross goblins waiting for them?

Fortunately, there seemed to be no one in sight as they came of out the portal next to the frozen lake they had seen inside the snow globe. "Lucky for us we didn't come out ten feet to the right," Alex said, forcing a smile. "I'd hate to test how thick that ice is."

Before Noah could say anything, they heard a soft tinkling sound. They looked to the nearby cabin and saw two majestic reindeer staring right at them. One was shaking its head back and forth; a small bell attached to one of its antlers was chiming lightly with each toss.

"I see you've met my security system," a creaky voice said from behind them. "I was wondering if you two would turn up here."

The boys turned to see a friendly-looking woman smiling brightly. She had long silver hair in a braid down to her waist, and she wore a brilliantly colored dress that reminded the boys of the clothes they had seen the elves wearing. Her skin was fine like tissue paper, and many wrinkles told the boys that she was quite old, but her eyes, the color of sapphires, seemed full of life and wisdom.

"Well, you had best come inside then," the old woman said kindly. "My name is Eveline, and you two are very welcome in my home." She then headed toward the charming little cabin that seemed right out of a fairy tale book. Warm lights glowed from inside while white smoke puffed merrily from the chimney.

Noah noticed that the woman was holding a large bundle of wood. "Let me take that for you," he said.

She stopped and smiled, then let him take the wood from her. "Ah, it seems your parents have raised you well. I am so glad to see that. True kindness is increasingly rare these days, but it is the most important quality a person can have."

65

The boys followed her in, the reindeer watching them the whole time. The inside of the cabin was even cheerier than the outside. A warm fire crackled inside a wood-burning stove, and the boys could smell delicious hints of cinnamon and gingerbread in the air.

Noah laid the wood down while Eveline went straight to the kitchen, returning a moment later with a tray of hot cocoa and fresh-baked cookies. "Oh my gosh, this is just like the hot chocolate at the hotel," Alex said as he took a sip from his steaming mug.

"Where do you think they got the recipe?" the woman said with a wink.

The boys finally felt a little relaxed as they enjoyed the cookies and cocoa quietly, but after a while, Alex interrupted the silence. "Look, we really appreciate you letting us in and feeding us, but we're here to find our parents, and Neethermire said you could help us."

"I have avoided this fight so far, but I can no longer stand by and hope for a peaceful resolution. I will do what I can to help," Eveline said, a look of sadness creeping into her face.

"I don't mean to be rude, but if you're such good friends with Santa, why haven't you been tossed in jail with the rest of his supporters? Alex asked. "And Neethermire said that this place was in the North Pole, but why doesn't it look like the place we were earlier, where it was all dark and spooky?"

"Well, the answer to the second question is easy, so I'll start with that one. I live on the far east end of the North Pole, while Santa's village is on the west side. I like to be alone, so I choose to live out here with just my reindeer, Earl and Erma, for company. Eventually, the decay will reach these parts, but it will be some days yet."

"How about the first question?" Alex asked. "Why haven't they come for you?"

"Well, that's a harder question to answer, at least a more painful one. I guess it's because my son won't let them take me."

"Your son?" both boys said in unison.

"Yes, I have two sons," Eveline said with a deep sadness. "Malachi is my oldest son, and Nicolaus, or Santa Claus, as you know him, is my youngest."

The boys both nodded their heads in understanding as they saw the tears in Eveline's eyes. They were asking her to help them against her own son, and while she said she would help, they knew it would be very hard for her.

"Malachi wasn't always this way, you know," Eveline said as she dabbed at her eyes with her sleeve. "We used to be such a happy family. When the boys were growing up, they were inseparable. They were always planning adventures and exploring wherever they could. They really were the best of friends."

"So, what happened?" Alex asked. "How do you go from being best buds to tossing your brother in jail?"

"Ah, well that's a long story, but I suppose we have time before the others arrive," Eveline said.

"Others?" Noah asked.

"Well of course there are others. You didn't think that two boys and one old woman could take down an army, did you?" She chuckled to herself. "Just let me light the beacon." And with that, she moved to the wood stove and tossed a small, chalky blue ball inside. As she closed the door to the stove, the boys could see blue smoke billowing upward, where it would soon puff out from the chimney. "That should do it. The rest will come when they've seen my smoke sign," Eveline said.

When Eveline sat back down, she took a deep breath and then began her story. "As I said before, Malachi was very different many years ago when the boys were still young. He was happy and full of life. Everyone who knew him loved him. It wasn't until he and his brother found the crystal that things began to change."

Noah gulped and pulled the crystal from his pocket. "You mean like this one?" he asked.

"Yes, just like that one," she replied as a quick look of sorrow clouded her face. "As far as we know, there are only two in existence. The one in your hand, and the one Nicolaus controls. He uses his crystal to harness a small portion of Christmas magic to keep the North Pole running and ensure that Christmas is delivered every year.

"Malachi and Nick were not much older than yourselves when they found the crystal one fateful morning. They were climbing in the mountains near our small village in Switzerland when, as the boys described it, a crag on the hillside suddenly filled with light. When they looked inside, they saw the crystal pulsing like a heart."

"Whoa, that's just like what happened to me," Noah said. He let out a deep breath. "Except the crystal I found was hidden away in a river."

"Yeah, and it was different because you didn't share it with your brother," Alex grumbled. "I mean, if it was me that found a magic crystal, I would have shown it to you right away, not kept it a secret for two years."

"I didn't know it was magic," Noah said defensively. "Yes, I saw it glowing, but then it had gone out so quickly that I thought maybe my eyes were playing tricks on me. I thought I imagined it. It never did anything else until earlier today, when Izzy tricked us into following her into that trap."

Eveline cleared her throat, stopping the boys from bickering. "You mustn't let the crystal divide you. Remember that if you remember nothing else," she said, staring intently at the boys. "The crystals only make themselves known to brothers, and this one has chosen you, Alex and Noah James."

"But why us?" Noah asked as he rubbed the crystal instinctively.

"No one knows why a set of brothers is chosen, but what is certain is that the crystal you now hold contains great magic that can only be used by the brothers who found it. The one you have found is just reawakening after sleeping for many years, but sooner or later it will test you. You are both destined for great things, but take the advice that Malachi would not. No matter what happens, you must remain strong in your love and loyalty to one another."

Before Eveline could say anything else, a booming thump sounded on the heavy wood door. Both Noah and Alex jumped, but Eveline got up calmly and moved to the entry. She opened the door to reveal a massive polar bear standing on her porch.

AN ANSWERED CALL

The boys looked nervously at each other until the huge white bear picked Eveline up like a doll, wrapping her in his shaggy arms with a warmth that showed the two were old friends.

"Now that's a bear hug," Noah said with a laugh.

"Uh, bad joke, dude," Alex said, but at least he was smiling. "How about this one. What do you call a polar bear with no teeth?" Alex whispered so as not to offend the big bear.

"What?" Noah replied.

"A gummy bear. Get it?" Alex said as he elbowed Noah lightly in the ribs.

The boys were still chuckling when the bear set Eveline back on her feet. He turned his attention to Noah and Alex.

"You should know that polar bears have excellent hearing," the huge white bear said, looking at the boys sternly.

Noah and Alex were embarrassed and mumbled nervous apologies. After a moment, the bear broke out into a huge smile and began laughing so loud it shook the forest around them. "Actually, it was a rather good joke. You must be Alex and Noah," he said with a deep voice, bowing his head slightly to the boys. "I am Arnan, Chief of the Polar Bear Clans of the North Pole and a faithful supporter of Santa Claus. My clans are at your service, Sons of the Crystal."

"Pleased to meet you," Alex said, extending a hand to the giant bear. With a surprising gentleness, Arnan shook Alex's hand with his paw, then turned to do the same with Noah.

"Come now, let's get back inside. Malachi has spies everywhere," Eveline said, scanning the tree line. Just as she was about to close the door, she heard a voice nearby.

"Not so fast, Mama Claus," an artic fox said as she emerged slowly from the mound of snow that had camouflaged her. "Don't leave me out in the cold."

"Athena, how good to see you," Eveline said cooly to the fox; however, the look on her face said that it was anything but good to see the creature that had just appeared. "When I lit the beacon, I did not expect you to answer my call. Why have you come?" Eveline's voice was thick with suspicion.

73

"I have my reasons," Athena the fox said as she shook snow from her fur. "Don't worry, Mama Claus, I'm on your side. And from the look of it, you're going to need all the help you can get. Is this all the support you've managed to gather?"

"Not all the support," a small voice squeaked, drawing everyone's attention to a small mouse scurrying toward them. The mouse was wearing large spectacles, but still managed to run straight into Eveline's feet as if he couldn't see her.

"Why hello, Emmett." Eveline laughed as she picked up the mouse gently. "It's so good to see you again, old friend."

"I wish I could say the same, but I can barely see anything these days," the mouse said with a chuckle. "But even so, I've answered your call . . . and brought a few of Santa's friends with me as well."

Just then, a line of creatures big and small emerged from the nearby forest. There were hundreds more mice, dozens of white rabbits, a large pack of arctic wolves, and a few more reindeer. Flying above the line were twenty or more snowy owls, who seemed to scan the area as their wings pushed them majestically through the air.

"But how did you get here so quickly?" Eveline asked with amazement as she watched the small army of creatures coming toward them.

"News travels fast, and once it reached my rather large ears that the boys were in the North Pole earlier today, I started gathering those who remain steadfastly loyal to Santa," Emmett said. "We've actually just been waiting in your woods for you to light the beacon if the boys showed up here."

Eveline gave Emmett a gentle kiss on his tiny head. The boys had stood quietly, watching the procession of animals, but they could no longer contain their wonder at seeing so many amazing creatures.

Noah and Alex stepped from the porch and began walking among the animals that had finally reached the cabin. The mice whispered to each other, staring at the boys in awe. The rabbits bounced excitedly, while the wolves and reindeer watched the boys curiously. The owls, perched on tree branches above, ignored the boys as they continued to search the surrounding area for any signs of trouble.

After a few moments, the pack leader of the wolves approached the boys. "Is it true what they say? Are you two really Sons of the Crystal?" the wolf asked as he leaned in and sniffed the brothers.

"Uh, we don't know," Noah said nervously as the wolf circled him and Alex. "I mean, everyone keeps calling us that, but we don't really know what's going on. We're just trying to find our parents."

"Just as I thought," the wolf said with a low growl. "I had to see them for myself, but these are just boys. We will help free Santa Claus, but I will not risk my pack for these children."

As the wolf spoke, Noah could feel an intense heat forming inside the pocket where he kept his crystal. He tried to ignore it, but the warmth became so much that it began to burn his skin through his clothes. The crystal wanted to be seen. Noah had no choice but to pull it from its hiding place. As he did, white light shot into the air just as it had before.

"Forgive me," the wolf said as he bowed to the boys. Alex and Noah looked around to see all of the other animals bowing as well. "My pack is at your service, Sons of the Crystal."

Alex and Noah shared an uneasy glance. Yes, they had the crystal, and obviously it had power, but surely there was nothing special or magical about them . . . they were just the James brothers. "If it means they'll help us get Mom and Dad, let them call us anything they want," Alex whispered.

Nodding in agreement, Noah put the now-cool crystal back in his pocket. Just then, an owl perched in the tallest tree began to screech loudly. The sound was echoed by the other owls, and soon the woods were filled with loud noise that was clearly signaling danger.

The boys turned to look for Eveline, who was rushing toward them with Arnan the polar bear and Athena the fox just behind her. One of the owls swooped down and spoke quietly but urgently to Eveline.

"Malachi is here," Eveline said to Noah and Alex when she reached them, her face a mix of worry and sadness. "I will meet him and buy as much time as I can, but you two must get to Santa's village. Arnan will lead you."

Before she could say anything else, goblins began to emerge from the surrounding forests. From both the left and right sides came small armies of the fierce little creatures. The enemy was closing in too quickly for Noah to open a portal. The only way to escape was to go straight ahead, across the frozen lake.

Noah and Alex started to run for the lake, but seconds later felt the antlers of Earl and Erma, the reindeer, scooping them up and tossing them onto their backs. The boys leaned forward and held on to the reindeer's antlers with all their strength as they raced across the frozen water.

With Arnan and Athena running swiftly by their sides, the boys turned around to see the enemy following them onto the lake. The goblins slipped and slid across the ice, but still, they were not too far behind the boys and their companions. The way the creatures fell all over each other would have been funny if the boys hadn't been so scared.

"We'll never put enough distance between us to get through a portal," Alex shouted.

Knowing Alex was right, Noah wished that they could somehow find a way to escape. In that instant, Noah felt the heat of the crystal against his skin again. He pulled it from his pocket and saw the crystal glowing with a red light he hadn't seen before. Instinctively, he pointed the crystal at the frozen lake as a red ray of light shot forth.

The ice behind them began to break apart as it became clear that the crystal was melting the frozen lake. The creatures behind them recognized what was happening too late, as one by one they began falling through weakened spots in the ice. The boys just managed to make it to the other side as the last of the ice melted, and all the enemies behind them were plunged into the lake's dark waters.

Having escaped their pursuers, Noah and Alex climbed from the backs of Earl and Erma. They hugged the reindeer and thanked them for their help, then sent them back to protect Eveline.

"Open a portal," Alex said anxiously as the reindeer reluctantly left in search of their mistress.

"I don't know how to get to Santa's village," Noah said with panic in his voice. "Neethermire said to picture where you want to go, but I don't have any idea what it really looks like."

"Remember the snow globes at the fireplace in the hotel? The first one I picked up had Santa's workshop inside. That should take us to the right place," Alex said impatiently.

"I didn't really look at that one," Noah said quietly, looking down at his feet so he didn't have to see the disappointment in everyone's eyes.

"A suggestion, young masters," Arnan's deep voice interrupted. "Perhaps Alex should give it a try. I don't know anything about this magic, but he has seen the village, so maybe he can get us there."

Noah shoved his hand in his pocket and clutched the crystal tightly. "It probably won't work for you anyway," he said under his breath. He knew he was being foolish, but he hesitated briefly before handing the crystal over to Alex. Having the crystal always made Noah feel special, even before he knew it had magic. He knew he should let Alex try, but it was hard to let go of the treasure he had kept secret for so long.

"Um, I don't want to rush this awkward brother moment," Athena interrupted, "but we've got company."

Sure enough, the boys saw two new groups of creatures rushing toward them through the trees, many more goblins on each side of the melted lake.

"Here goes nothing," Alex said as he closed his eyes and tried to concentrate on the scene that had been inside the snow globe. He recalled the rich wood tables where colorful toys were being crafted by dozens of elves. He thought of the vibrant hues and magical feel that had so intrigued him when he first looked at the snow globe.

He didn't feel anything happen, but when he opened his eyes again, he saw that a portal had opened nearby. "I did it," Alex said excitedly, pumping his fist in the air before running toward the opening.

The others followed and waited anxiously for the portal to close as the goblins got closer. Noah turned to his brother to take back the crystal; he didn't feel right not having it. The last thing Noah saw before the light overtook them was Alex slipping the crystal into his own pocket.

10

SANTA'S WORKSHOP

As they traveled through the portal, Noah tried not to be annoyed about Alex pocketing the crystal. "Of course he'll give it back," Noah said to himself. He shifted his thoughts to the workshop and what they might find when they exited the portal. As far as they knew, Malachi was near Eveline's cabin, but maybe he would have left guards behind.

However, Noah was relieved when they came out of the portal to find themselves alone in Santa's workshop. The place looked totally abandoned.

The huge workshop was filled with thick wood tables that were covered with unfinished toys, as if elves had left right in the middle of their work. There were teddy bears and dolls with the stuffing only halfway inside. Video game systems and other electronic toys were a mess, with wires sticking out all over the place.

Noah picked up a little car that was dull and gray. Sitting next to the car was a small pot with a paintbrush. It was filled with paint the color of ash. Scattered across the table were many other pots of paint, but all of them were gray, as if the color had been sucked right out of them. Like the forest they had seen earlier in the day, the workshop was void of life and color. It wasn't at all how Alex had seen it in the globe.

"I can't believe we are actually in Santa's workshop. This is crazy," Alex said, forgetting for just a moment the danger they were in. He and Noah looked around and saw the floor was littered with miniature hot air balloons and small toy airplanes. "I bet those are normally floating around up there," Alex said, pointing to the soaring ceilings. "I guess without Santa's magic, they can't fly."

"It's just so sad," said Noah. "I wonder what it's like normally?"

"It's the most magical place on the planet," Athena replied, so quietly the boys almost didn't hear her. They turned to look at the fox, and could see a look of sadness on her face that she quickly replaced with a scowl. "C'mon, we're not here for sightseeing. We've got a mission," she said gruffly.

84

"The rumors are that Santa and the rest of the prisoners are being held in the dungeons below the command center," Arnan said. "It's likely your parents will be there too. The problem is the command center is on the other side of the village, at least a fifteen-minute walk from here."

"Well, let's go!" Alex said, heading for the exit.

"Not so fast, little prince," Athena said, cutting the boys off from the door. "You two aren't going to get very far. We might have gotten lucky here, but there's no way the rest of the village will be this empty."

"She's right," agreed Arnan. "Malachi is not stupid; he will have his minions looking for you."

"I have an idea," said Noah as he turned and dashed away to a nearby wall, where several elves' robes hung from wooden pegs. "Here. We can put these on, and if we don't draw any attention to ourselves, maybe we can blend in. We didn't know Izzy was an elf, right?"

"You're right," Alex said excitedly. "Neethermire said the elves' features don't develop until they get older. Izzy looked just like another kid . . . well, except for those eyes of hers," he said, looking a little troubled.

"It might work," Athena said, then paused. "And it sounds like the only chance we have, but we must go now. Once Malachi realizes you aren't at Eveline's cabin, he will come straight back here. I can blend in with the snow and go with them, but Arnan, there is no way you can move about unseen. You will have to stay here."

"There is no way I am leaving the boys to you, fox," Arnan said heatedly. "The last I heard, you were banned from the village. I promised Eveline that I would protect the boys, and I intend to do just that."

"I have paid my debt," Athena snarled in response. "What happened is between me and Santa Claus. Yes, he and I had our disagreements, but I remain his loyal servant. I am here to make things right."

"I believe her," Noah said softly, seeing a deep sorrow in Athena's eyes. "And she is right, Arnan. There is no way you can go unnoticed. We have to take a chance."

"Here, take my walkie-talkie," Alex said as he pulled the device from his jacket. He handed it to Arnan and showed him quickly how to work it. "If we get in trouble, we'll call you right away."

"Wait!" Noah said excitedly, taking out his walkie-talkie. "I wonder if we are close enough to Mom and Dad again to be in range." He switched to the channel the boys used to communicate with their parents. "Mom, Dad, come in. This is Noah. Do you copy?" he said, then waited a moment before he repeated the words again three times.

Disappointment washed over Noah when he was met with nothing but static. He started putting the walkie-talkie away when he heard the unmistakable sound of his mother's voice.

"Noah! This is Mom. Are you and Alex OK?" Anna asked frantically.

"We're OK, Mom," both boys said in response.

"Are you and Dad alright?" Alex asked, his voice trembling like he might cry.

The next voice they heard was their father's. "We're going to be just fine, guys. What's important now is that you boys stay safe. Where are you?" Edward whispered as if there might be someone nearby that he didn't want to hear him.

"We're close," Noah said, his heart lifted at hearing that both of his parents were unharmed. "We're coming to get you!"

Edward began to say something, but fell silent instantly. "And what do we have here?" the boys heard someone say. It sounded like the owner of the voice was standing right next to their parents. "Give it here," the voice said in a vicious tone.

The next thing the boys heard was the sound of a struggle. They could hear their dad fighting with someone or something. Suddenly Anna's voice was breaking through, yelling, "Do not come here, boys! Run, run!" The last thing the boys heard was a noise like a howl followed by a loud thud. Then all went silent.

11

A DARK DUNGEON

"We've got to go, now!" Alex yelled as he threw a robe over his clothes. "There is no time to plan. You guys heard that. Mom and Dad are in serious trouble."

Noah agreed and pulled a robe on as well. The boys headed for the exit with Athena right behind them. "It's time to find out what else this thing can do," Alex said as he pulled the crystal from his pocket and walked out the door.

Noah didn't like that Alex still had the crystal. He had to fight the urge to snatch it back from his brother, but in that moment, the only thing that mattered was getting to their parents.

Noah and Athena followed Alex, while Arnan stayed behind reluctantly. Athena, being true to her word, disappeared behind a snow pile almost at once. She was so good at camouflaging herself that the boys only knew where she was when they could hear her voice.

Athena directed them to the command center, reminding them often to keep their heads down or to slow their pace so they didn't stand out. It turned out that her warnings were unnecessary, as they didn't pass a single elf or any other creature as they made their way through the village.

"This is so weird," Noah said. "This place feels like a ghost town."

"Maybe Malachi took all of his crew with him to Eveline's. And I'm guessing the elves that are loyal to Santa are probably hiding so they don't get thrown in jail too," Alex said. He agreed with his brother that the emptiness of the village seemed odd, but they had no other choice than to go after their mom and dad. Alex knew his parents wouldn't hesitate to save him and his brother, so he wouldn't hesitate either, no matter how scared he was.

When they reached the command center, Athena emerged from her hiding place. She led the boys to an entrance she said was nearest the prison cells. They entered the building slowly, keeping their heads down and trying to blend in, but again, it was unnecessary, as there was no one in sight.

"This is too easy," Noah said quietly. "Where is everybody?"

"I know, I don't like it either," Alex said.

The boys looked around, feeling like they had stepped into a tech company rather than the center of a magical village. The walls of the building were broken into three levels and were mostly covered by computers and screens. In the center of the room was a raised octagonal stage, where a huge hologram display of the earth spun slowly.

As the model of the earth rotated, Noah noticed that there were glowing red dots on several major cities, including New York, Paris, London, Tokyo, and multiple others. "I wonder what those red dots are for?" Noah whispered.

"I don't know, but look at this," Alex said as he studied a nearby computer screen. On the display was an image of what was clearly a weapon, but it was unlike anything the boys had seen before. It reminded them of something that would be in a sci-fi movie. The weapon itself was a large, clear globe mounted at an angle. The inside of the globe was filled with streams of light that looked like a plasma ball the boys had seen at their local science center. Attached to one side of the globe was a long point that looked like the tip of a ray gun.

"Look, I don't know what Malachi is up to," Athena interrupted, "but we don't have time for this. The only person who stands a chance of stopping him is locked up, so we've got to move!"

The fox led the way and the boys followed cautiously. They went down a long corridor until they finally arrived at a massive wood door that was carved with a strange symbol. "They're down there, through that door," Athena said.

A huge lock ensured the door would not be easily opened. The three looked around for a key nearby but found nothing. Just then, the crystal, which Alex was still gripping tightly, began to glow. However, this time it radiated a bright blue light.

"I wonder what the blue light means?" Noah said quietly. "The red light obviously makes heat, the way it melted that lake, and I think the white light is the crystal's way of saying hello or that it wants to be seen."

"I don't know, but stand back and let's find out," Alex said nervously. He pointed the crystal at the lock, and was shocked when a tiny bolt of blue light shot from its tip. The lock froze and then fell to the ground with a loud clang that echoed down the hallway.

"Well, if they didn't know we were here, they do now!" Noah said as he moved quickly to the door. "C'mon, help me. This thing is insanely heavy." He panted as he struggled to budge the door. Alex and Athena rushed to help, and very slowly, they were able to open it.

"Be careful," Athena whispered. "We don't know who or what else is down there."

The crystal, which was still glowing blue, immediately went out as soon as they walked through the door. "Huh, what happened?" Alex asked as he shook the crystal, trying to turn it back on. "We need this thing working if we're going down there." He gestured to the dark dungeons below, which were only dimly lit by torches scattered along the walls.

"Here, give it to me," Noah said, putting out his hand to take back the crystal. Noah wasn't sure if he was imagining it, but it seemed that Alex paused before giving it back.

Noah felt a sense of relief at having the crystal back in his hands again. He closed his eyes, focused his thoughts, and pictured the crystal glowing again, but when he opened his eyes, he saw that nothing had happened.

"Nice job, hot shot," Alex joked.

"It's not you," Athena said. "Santa had this prison sealed so that no magic could be used beyond that door, not even his own. Whatever we're going to face down there, we're going to have to do it without the help of that crystal."

Noah gulped. "OK, let's go get Mom and Dad," he said, although he didn't feel very brave now that he knew the crystal wouldn't be able to help them if they got in trouble.

The three made their way silently down the steps. At the bottom, they came to an empty cell to the right that looked like it had been recently occupied. A tray of half-eaten food and a crumpled red velvet coat sat abandoned in the corner. "Santa was here," Athena whispered. "I'd know that coat anywhere. But the question is, where is he now?" She scanned the cell for any other clues, but found none.

Up ahead, they could see a light in the distance casting shadows on the walls.

"OK, follow me," Athena said. She padded stealthily through the dark passageway, with the boys close behind her. As they drew closer to the light, they could make out voices up ahead in an alcove to the right. They continued to move closer, and soon they could see a set of keys hanging on the wall just outside the nook where the light was coming from.

"It's not fair is all I'm saying," said one particularly whiny voice. The speaker sounded as though they might have a very stuffed-up nose. "I mean, why do we have to stay here doing all the guarding while everyone else is off hunting those human boys? These cells don't even need guarding at all if you ask me."

Noah, Alex, and Athena crept closer and could see that the speaker was a very chubby goblin. He was talking to another goblin, who seemed to be half asleep, having not paid attention at all to what his companion had said.

"Did you hear me?" said the first, knocking the other goblin upside the head with a chunk of bread he had been chewing on.

In answer, the second goblin grabbed a club lying next to him and swung it wildly, missing the first goblin all together. The next thing the boys knew, the goblins were locked in a wild wrestling match, tussling all over the floor.

"Now is our chance," Alex whispered, hoping the goblins would be too busy fighting to notice them pass. Sure enough, the boys and Athena moved quickly, and were able to grab the set of keys while avoiding being seen by the jailers, who were otherwise occupied with their brawl.

The three continued past the struggling creatures and followed the passageway for a few minutes. They passed several cells along the way that seemed empty before they came to a large, dark cell on the left of the corridor. The door to the cell was secured with a large lock, and they thought they could see faint movement toward the back of the chamber.

"Mom, Dad? Are you in there?" Noah whispered as he scanned the black cell for any sign of his parents.

From the darkness, they heard a muffled sound that they couldn't make out.

"Just open it," Alex said anxiously. "Mom and Dad could be in there."

Noah tried several keys but finally got the right one, and the lock sprung open.

The boys walked cautiously toward the back of the cell while Athena quickly disappeared into the shadows. Noah and Alex followed the muffled sound, which got louder and more insistent as they drew closer.

Noah almost dropped the keys when, seconds later, he saw two hunched shapes moving on the ground just ahead of them. As the boys got closer, they could see it was their parents, who were frantically struggling against the restraints that held them. Their ankles and wrists were bound with ropes and they were gagged with duct tape. Anna shook her head wildly, her screams stifled behind the tape as she desperately tried to tell the boys something.

Alex reached down and ripped the duct tape from her mouth as Noah did the same for their father. "Behind you!" both Anna and Edward yelled at the same time.

Noah and Alex turned to see the two fat jailers smiling wickedly at them. Each holding a huge club in their gnarled hands, they were completely blocking the door to the cell. There was no way out.

12

GREEDY GOBLINS

"Well Carl, looky what we have here," the first goblin said to the other as he wiped a small amount of blood from his mouth with the sleeve of his dirty shirt.

"Ha! I knew it!" the creature called Carl said, rubbing a lump that was rapidly growing on his forehead. "I knew those brothers would show up here. Didn't I tell you that we'd be stupid to go out hunting them when they'd walk right into our hands if we just stayed near their pathetic little parents? Didn't I say that, Dale?" Carl said, elbowing his partner in the ribs.

"No, you idiot. You said just the opposite not even five minutes ago. You were whining that we were stuck here, missing out on all the action. Remember that?" Dale said, rolling his eyes.

Carl stared hard at Dale; it looked like the two goblins might start fighting again at any moment. But instead, they turned their attention back to the boys and their parents, who were still on the floor trying unsuccessfully to free themselves from their restraints.

"C'mon, let's get them upstairs," Carl said roughly. "Malachi is going to want to see them as soon as he gets back. Just imagine the reward he's gonna have in store for us."

"What about their parents and that other one?" Dale asked, nodding his head toward a small shape in the far corner of the cell.

From the darkness, the boys could just make out a pair of glowing green eyes.

"Izzy!" Alex said to himself as his heart leapt a little. He started to move toward her, but was stopped as the goblins forcefully grabbed the two boys by their arms.

"Leave them here to rot," Carl laughed cruelly. "Who knows what Malachi has planned for the humans, but I know that little elf is worthless to us now."

And with that, the goblins started pushing the boys back toward the entrance of the cell as their parents fought harder still to free themselves.

"Get your hands off our kids!" Edward yelled. He tried to sound as forceful as he could, but there was nothing he could do but watch as his boys were marched from the cell. He and Anna had tried everything they could to loosen their bonds, but they wouldn't budge.

Edward and Anna continued to shout as Noah, Alex, and their captors disappeared from their view. "Shh," they heard a voice whisper. From the darkness emerged an all-white fox. "I'm a friend of your boys. My name is Athena," the fox whispered as Edward and Anna looked at each other uneasily.

"Can you free us?" Anna asked hopefully. But instead of answering, Athena bared her sharp teeth and went straight for Edward's ropes. Within no time, Athena had sliced through the bonds and Edward was free and running from the cell.

"I'm going after them!" he said quietly as Athena got to work on Anna's restraints.

"I'm right behind you," Anna said, but Edward was already gone.

"Don't forget the girl," Anna said to Athena as the fox finished chewing through the ropes. Edward and Anna had been aware that the girl was in the cell with them, but every time they tried to talk to her, she had remained silent and scooted away from them. They assumed she was afraid and had finally left her alone.

Once free, Anna ran from the cell and down the corridor just in time to see Edward ducking into an alcove and emerging with two clubs, just like the goblins had been holding. Anna caught up to him, and he tossed one of the weapons back to her without breaking stride.

They ran on and saw the boys and goblins up ahead at the base of the stairs. The boys were moving as slowly as they could while the jailers made threats to keep them walking. "You know what goblins like to eat more than anything?" Carl asked menacingly.

"By the smell of your breath, I'd say it was cat poop," Alex said. Noah laughed, and even Dale struggled not to chuckle.

Carl looked enraged, but before he could do anything, Edward was upon them. "I said, get your hands off my kids!" Edward roared as he swung his club hard, hitting Carl squarely in the jaw. Carl dropped like a fly, then Edward turned to Dale, who was attempting to run away.

"Not so fast," said Anna as she blocked his retreat. While the goblins were big enough to manhandle the boys, a full-grown adult was another matter. Dale cowered and looked like he might cry. "Give me your keys," Anna demanded.

Dale quickly handed the keys over, and didn't argue a bit as Edward shoved him into the nearest cell. They dragged the unconscious Carl in as well and locked the door.

With the goblins locked up, Anna and Edward moved quickly to the boys and hugged them as tightly as they could. "Thank goodness you guys are OK! We were so worried about you two," Anna said with tears in her eyes.

Just then, Izzy and Athena came running up. "I hate to break up this Hallmark family moment, but we've got to find Santa and get out of here. Do you know where he is?" Athena asked, looking at Edward and Anna.

"Santa?" Edward said, clearly confused. "Look, the last thing we remember was waiting for the boys at the base of the North Point Mountain when we were ambushed by at least twenty of whatever those creatures are." He gestured toward the goblins in the cell. "Anna and I were both knocked unconscious by those savage little things. When we woke up, we found ourselves here. The jailers didn't say a thing to us until they heard us talking to you boys on the walkie-talkie. That's when they tied us up and covered our mouths with the duct tape."

"Umm, look. We're going to tell you guys something that is going to be really hard to believe, but try to keep an open mind," Alex said. He and Noah then proceeded to fill their parents in on all that had happened since they last saw each other.

When they reached the end of the story, their parents hugged them again. "You boys have been so brave," was all Edward had a chance to say before Athena interrupted again.

"OK, now that everybody knows everything, we really gotta go," the fox said impatiently, then started up the stairs. "Santa's not going to save himself!"

"Wait," Izzy said shyly, speaking for the first time. The boys had forgotten about her in their excitement at seeing their parents. "There are a ton more of Santa's supporters who are locked up down here. The cells beyond where we were held are full of elves and animals alike. We have to set them free." Izzy was unable to look at Alex or Noah. "I know I don't have the right to ask anything of you guys, but I am begging you to save my parents."

Neither Alex nor Noah hesitated before telling Izzy that of course they would help her.

Izzy burst into tears at the boys' kindness toward her. Even after she had betrayed them, they were still willing to help her. "If it wasn't for me, you guys wouldn't be in this mess," she said, tears running down her face.

"We understand, and we forgive you," Noah said kindly. "We would have done the same for our parents."

"OK, enough of this," Athena said coldly. "If it will get this show on the road, I will go back and release everyone. Just give me the keys."

The others tried to protest that they should go too, but Athena stopped them. "I'm the fastest, and I'm pretty sure I'm the only one that can see well in the dark. You guys head back and find Arnan; he should have an idea of a safe place for you to go," she said. "Although I'm not sure anywhere is safe right now," she added as an afterthought before taking the keys in her teeth and bounding off back down the dark tunnels.

"OK, let's go," Edward said as he led the way, his club held out in front of him. Anna, the boys, and Izzy followed him up the stairs and through the massive door that guarded the dungeon.

As soon as they were through the door, Noah felt a familiar warmth in his pocket. He pulled the crystal out, and sure enough, it was glowing again. He felt an instant sense of security knowing that he would be able to use it if he needed it. He was still staring at the crystal as they continued down the hall and back into the main room of the command center.

"It's about time," a deep voice said. Noah finally looked up and realized that what had been an empty room when they were there before was now full of goblins staring hard at him and his family. Within seconds, they were surrounded by more than twenty of the foul creatures, who were all holding various weapons.

"I was beginning to think you'd never make it out of the dungeons. I thought I was going to have to come down there after you," the voice continued with a cheerless laugh.

From the shadows stepped a very large, powerful-looking man. He was dressed in all black with a long fur-lined coat hanging down to his boots. With long white hair and a well-groomed beard, he could almost be Santa Claus. But the evil look in his eyes made it clear that he was not.

"Allow me to introduce myself," the man said as he strode toward the James family. "I am Malachi."

MALACHI

"What do you want with us?" asked Alex, stepping forward bravely.

"So bold," Malachi said with a hint of admiration in his voice. "You know, I was a bold boy too. When I saw something I wanted, I took it." He stared directly at Alex.

"And now, I want that crystal your brother is holding," Malachi said, turning his attention to Noah. "Just hand it over and I'll let you and your family go. You'll be home in time for Christmas . . . well, what will be left of Christmas. You have my word."

"But why do you want it?" Noah asked. "Eveline told us the only ones who can use its powers are the set of brothers that the crystal has chosen."

"Ah yes, my dear sweet mother. Well let's just say I want your crystal for preventative reasons," Malachi said smoothly. "And what else did my loving mother tell you boys about the crystal? Did she tell you how good old Saint Nick stole it from me? Did she tell you how I was destined to be Santa Claus and my brother swooped in and took the magic for himself? No, I don't imagine she got that far, did she?" he asked, anger flooding his face.

"You know what—better yet, let's have the traitor himself tell us the tale, shall we?" Malachi said. He nodded his head, and six goblins moved into the room, shoving a tied-up man before them.

The man was just as big as Malachi, and while he had similar thick white hair and a bushy beard, the look of goodness and strength in his eyes was completely different. He was wearing dirty red trousers held up by tattered suspenders and a ripped white shirt that looked stained with dirt and blood. The man could be none other than Santa Claus himself.

Noah and Alex shared a frightened look.

"Here he is. Here he is. I bet you boys always wanted to meet Santa, didn't you? C'mon, you can admit it," Malachi said mockingly. "Everyone wants to meet The Claus . . . so what do you think? Are you impressed?" He grabbed Santa roughly by the ropes that bound him and shoved him to his knees. "Now that you're where you belong, brother, why don't you tell these brothers what you did?"

Even on his knees, Santa looked regal as he stared at Malachi. "I love you, brother," Santa said with complete sincerity. "Please do not do this. All can be forgiven. Please, brother."

A strange sadness clouded Malachi's face, but it was quickly replaced with a sneer. He hesitated for only the briefest second, then spoke. "Oh no, brother. All cannot be forgiven. You took what was rightfully mine, and I will have it back. Whatever it takes."

Santa continued to speak with his brother, but the look of hope on his face was replaced with sadness. "The crystal chose me, brother," Santa said softly. "There are many days I wonder what would have happened if we had never found the crystal."

"We found the crystal?" Malachi roared, no longer trying to suppress the rage that was inside him. "It was me; I was the one that found the crystal. Do you remember that, or has your memory gone soft as well as your belly?" With that, Malachi lifted a heavy boot and kicked Santa hard, right in the stomach.

Santa doubled over at the blow, but quickly righted himself. "Yes, you saw the glow on the hillside first, but we climbed that cliff together, and together we brought the crystal home," Santa said as he looked imploringly at his brother. "The crystal chose both of us at first, but we were warned that eventually the powers would only be wielded by one of us when a new Santa was chosen."

Noah and Alex both listened intently to the argument between Santa and Malachi. Noah elbowed his brother and whispered nervously, "What are they saying? Does that mean that one of us is going to be the next Santa Claus?"

Alex shrugged his shoulders, but he was wondering the same thing. Eveline had told them there were only two crystals in the world and that each chose a set of brothers. She didn't mention the part where the crystal eventually chose only one of them. He felt very uneasy as he thought more about it. He looked over at his brother. Was he imagining it, or did Noah seem to be gripping the crystal extra tightly?

Alex's attention was pulled away from Noah and the crystal as Malachi roared, "Enough of these excuses!" He composed himself, then continued, "I've been doing some digging, and thanks to my goblin friends here, I've learned some very interesting information. It turns out the goblins are great keepers of records, just like the elves. I suppose it's in their blood, after all," Malachi said with a dark laugh.

"What's he talking about?" Noah whispered again, but this time Malachi heard him.

"Oh my, I've almost forgotten our guests," Malachi said, turning his attention from Santa back to the James family. "Yes, I'm sure all of this makes very little sense to you, but you see, these creatures all around you—these poor, ugly, misshapen little goblins—were once beautiful elves."

Noah could hear several of the goblins closest to them grunt with anger as Malachi described them in such unpleasant terms, but Malachi went on.

"Many, many years and several Santas ago, a group of elves became tired of working for Santa. Not that I blame them. I can't imagine doing such dreadfully boring work day in and day out. All holly jolly this and merry that. Anyway, those rebel elves led a revolt and tried to take over the North Pole.

"Of course, they failed miserably because they lacked strong leadership. The group of rogue elves was banished forever by the Santa Claus at the time, so they moved into the dark forests just outside the North Pole. Being cut off from Christmas magic, they began to mutate until they evolved into these hideous things you see today."

Again, Noah noticed that goblins around him seemed to seethe with anger as Malachi spoke. Noah wondered to himself if maybe the goblins were not as loyal to Malachi as the man thought.

"Anyway," Malachi continued, ignoring the grumbling goblins around him, "it turns out that several of the elves who were banished were keepers of the North Pole's ancient records. They have shared with me many intriguing things. I won't bore you with all the details, but I will share with you my favorite part." Malachi's eyes gleamed with anticipation.

With all attention on him, Malachi slowly pulled a crystal from his coat pocket. It looked just like the one Noah was holding, except it was not glowing. Malachi looked straight at Santa Claus. "It seems that while the crystal may have mistakenly chosen you, dear brother, you can make things right by transferring the crystal's power to me."

"You know I will never do that," Santa Claus said, looking his brother straight in the eyes.

"You can and you will," Malachi said cruelly. "And when you do, I will put my plans in motion." He gestured to the model of the earth the boys had seen when they entered earlier. "Thanks to the stealthy delivery system the North Pole already has in place, and the unsurpassed technology the elves have created, I plan to bring the world to its knees.

"The problem with you, Nick, is that you've always been a small thinker," Malachi continued. "I mean c'mon, you have the ability to infiltrate any place in the world undetected, and yet you have wasted these powers on giving children toys." He laughed.

"Oh well, once you transfer the power, I'll see just what is possible with the powers you have wasted. Now, bring me the boys!" Malachi commanded.

The goblins surrounding the James family prodded them roughly toward Malachi.

"Now, as I was saying, you will give me the power . . . or else," Malachi said, grabbing Noah by the arm and yanking him onto the stage in the center of the room. Malachi left Noah standing alone as he moved to a large control panel above the stage and entered several commands.

Noah watched anxiously as the hologram of the earth disappeared while Malachi continued to work the controls. A second later, Noah felt rumbling below his feet and looked down to see the floor parting slowly to reveal a hidden compartment below the stage. From the hole in the floor, a large, strange device was being slowly raised on a motorized platform. Noah realized with panic that it was the weapon they had seen in the diagram earlier . . . and it was pointed straight at him.

14

THE HAJE

Shaking with fear, Noah knew he had to do something. He didn't know what the weapon aimed at him could do, and he didn't want to find out. He gripped his crystal tightly, closed his eyes, and began to concentrate. The crystal began to glow red as he remembered the way it had melted the frozen lake earlier.

"I wouldn't do that if I were you," Malachi said menacingly. "Please take a look at your family and consider if attacking me will end well for those you love."

Noah looked over at his mom, dad, and Alex to see three goblins painfully pinning their arms behind their backs while other goblins held sharply pointed spears at their throats. There was no way he could risk something happening to his family, so he let the crystal's power go.

"Now that's a good boy," Malachi said mockingly. "I'm guessing you always do as you're told, don't you?"

Not waiting for an answer, Malachi turned back to Santa Claus and said, "My patience runs thin. You will transfer the powers of Christmas magic to me, or I will test my latest creation on good, kind Noah here. You know, he somewhat reminds me of you as a boy, so maybe I'll do it anyway." He chuckled darkly.

"Oh, I'm just kidding," Malachi continued. "I'm not a monster, after all. But perhaps you all would like a quick demonstration of what this wonder of technology can do. You see, I've only tried it a handful of times, but I think you'll all agree the results are quite astounding. Bring in the subjects!"

A side door in the command center opened, and five elves, one female and four males, were led onto the stage by a single goblin. It was obvious immediately that something was not right with the elves. Their skin seemed an ashen gray color and they all stared lifelessly straight ahead. Once lined up, they did not move, they did not resist; it was as if the lights were on, but no one was home inside their bodies.

"Mom! Dad!" Izzy cried from somewhere among the goblins. Noah looked at the elves on stage, then his gaze fell on the female. For the briefest second, it seemed as if Izzy's voice might have roused something in her, but she just took a deep breath and continued to stand motionless, her eyes dull. "What have you done to them?" Izzy yelled.

"A good question," Malachi said, fixing his cruel stare on Izzy. "Well, you see, I've been meaning to try out this new gadget for quite some time." He gestured toward the large weapon. "And you gave me the perfect excuse to start with your parents when you let the James brothers escape."

Alex tried to find Izzy in the crowd of goblins, although it was hard to move his head with a spear at his throat. When his eyes finally found her, he saw she was weeping uncontrollably, her small body shaking with sobs. He felt so bad for her, as he knew she already felt so much guilt about betraying him and his brother. To see her parents in such a state must be unbearable, he thought.

Alex turned his attention back to Malachi, who continued speaking. "I call it the HAJE, short for the Happiness And Joy Extractor. I won't bog you down with all the details, but basically it emits waves that block the brain from experiencing any sort of happiness or hope. The beautiful thing is that it works on all creatures. For now, I can only set it to affect a single individual. However, once my dear brother transfers the power of Christmas magic to me, I will be able to use the crystal to amplify the HAJE's energy to strike a whole forest, or even an entire city, with just one blast. Imagine that, a world without happiness, a world full of pain, an entire world of people and creatures just like me."

While Noah was keenly aware that the HAJE was still aimed at him, he suddenly felt very sorry for Malachi. He couldn't imagine living his life as Malachi had just described. He knew that Malachi hadn't always been bad. He had family who loved him even if he didn't want to admit it—but Malachi had chosen to let his feelings of betrayal and jealousy fester until all he could see was his own misery.

Noah's feelings of compassion for Malachi were interrupted as, suddenly, the HAJE began to hum as if it was starting up. Sure enough, Noah looked up at Malachi, who was operating the control panel and staring threateningly at Santa Claus. "This is your last chance, Nick. Agree to transfer the power, or I will use the weapon on the boy."

"I will do as you ask; I have no other choice. I cannot let a child suffer if I have the chance to stop it," Santa said solemnly.

"Good choice," Malachi said as he came down from the control booth. Several of the goblins pulled Santa to his feet and shuffled him toward Malachi without untying him. "Let's make this quick, shall we?"

"As you wish, brother." Santa shook his head with great sadness.

Malachi held out the crystal in front of him and instructed his brother to place his hands on it, as well. "All you have to do is repeat after me, and this will all be over," Malachi said excitedly. Then he spoke the words that the goblins had taught him from the ancient records.

Santa repeated the words. "Christmas magic, ancient light, powers I hold this very night. Brothers chosen long ago. Two sons to make the crystal glow. While I became the Santa Claus, I hereby declare by scared laws. That I give these powers, free and true. All the magic, I bestow on you."

A maniacal laugh rose in Malachi's throat as he shoved Santa backward and held the now-glowing crystal above his head. "Ha! It is mine," Malachi boomed. "I've waited for this moment for decades. As my first order of business, I think I'll tie up some loose ends." He pointed his crystal at Santa. "Now let's see what this thing can do!"

"Stop!" Noah screamed. "You got what you wanted, now let him go."

"Let him go? Let him go?" Malachi said cruelly. "Don't you know anything? I am the bad guy. I'm not sure what kind of movies you've been watching, but the bad guy never just lets people go. That goes for you and your annoying family as well. I'll deal with you when I'm done with my brother." Malachi pointed the crystal back at Santa.

Noah knew he had to take a chance, even with the knowledge that his family could be in danger. He gripped his crystal, willing the power to flow through it. It glowed with a deep red, but just as he was about to aim it at Malachi, a hurtling white shape came crashing into him. Athena the fox had come out of nowhere, knocking Noah roughly to the ground.

Before he could react, Athena yanked the crystal from his hand and ran toward Malachi. It looked as if she meant to give the crystal to the evil man. Noah couldn't believe he had trusted her; he had been so positive she was on their side.

If Malachi was distracted by the commotion, he didn't show it. His single focus was on Santa Claus. "Say goodbye, brother," he said just as a bright blue ray shot from the crystal's tip. It was aimed right at Santa's heart.

Noah watched as Athena bounded toward Malachi with his crystal in her mouth. However, instead of giving Malachi the crystal, she leapt at the last moment toward the blue ray. In one smooth movement, she managed to put herself between Santa and the blast of power from the crystal. She angled Noah's crystal perfectly so the ray from the first crystal hit the one in her mouth.

Noah watched helplessly as the light was refracted, sending hundreds of smaller, less intense blasts all over the room. Goblins were struck down, computer monitors were frozen, even the ceiling was hit multiple times. Noah looked over to see that his family had gotten loose from their captors in all the chaos. Izzy also appeared unharmed as she joined his parents and brother and began running toward him.

Noah's attention was pulled from his family as he realized pieces of the roof were crashing down around him. They needed to get out of there quickly before the whole place came down. He looked over and saw Santa standing over Athena, who lay crumpled on the floor, her white body pressed beneath a beam that had fallen from the ceiling. His hands still tied up, Santa tried to shove the large beam off her with his feet, but it would not budge.

Noah ran to Santa and untied him just as his family joined them. "We've got to go! Now!" Edward said.

"I won't leave her," Santa said.

Knowing that he meant it, Edward and Anna immediately got to work trying to help Santa get the beam off Athena. They had almost freed her when Alex looked over and saw Malachi's boots peeking out from beneath some rubble. He didn't know if Malachi had been struck by one of the crystal's rays or if he had been knocked down by falling debris, but Alex could see that he was moving only slightly.

Without thinking, Alex ran over and grabbed Santa's crystal from Malachi's hand. Just as he began to run away, a powerful hand grabbed his ankle, knocking him to the ground and almost forcing him to drop the crystal.

Alex could see Malachi's eyes from under the rubble. The man was definitely hurt, and beyond angry. Alex shook his foot free and headed back to his family just as Santa hoisted Athena's limp body over his shoulder and ran toward the door.

Alex handed Santa his crystal without breaking stride, then looked back toward Malachi one last time as he followed everyone toward the exit. His breath caught as he realized that Malachi was no longer buried under debris. He was gone!

Alex scanned the room as the building continued to crumble around them. He was almost to the door when he caught sight of Malachi's black cloak just as the man disappeared into the hole in the floor that the HAJE had come out of.

The goblins had scattered at the first sign of danger, leaving behind their fallen brothers to fend for themselves. The five elves, including Izzy's parents, stood unmoving as the building crashed down around them. Izzy took her mother's hand and led her out. The other four followed, narrowly escaping a large beam that would have crushed them all.

Once outside, Noah didn't hesitate before opening a portal.

15

SANTA CLAUS

Moments later, the group found themselves in the water park back at the North Point Ski Resort.

"You brought us back here?" Alex asked with disbelief. "Maybe you forgot that the last time we were here, Neethermire was being attacked by a whole squad of goblins!"

"It was the first place I thought of," Noah said defensively. "I'm getting a little sick of you questioning everything I do. Where would you have taken us, genius?" Noah's feelings were clearly hurt.

Before Alex could answer, Santa interrupted. He laid a gentle hand on Noah's shoulder, then said, "You were right to bring us here, Noah. This is as safe as any place right now. And we have many resources here. The truth is, I don't know the extent of Malachi's influence yet. At this point, there are few I can truly trust. Speaking of those I can trust, you say that Neethermire was under attack when last you saw him?"

The boys both nodded their heads.

"Well, if there is one thing I can be certain of, it is that Neethermire is likely to have had the upper hand in any battle, no matter the odds he faced."

"Well, it appears I'm not too old to blush. You honor me, Sir," a voice said. It was Neethermire, who was coming down the steep hill that led to the Avalanche waterslide, where Noah had received the weird message the night before. "I figured I'd wait things out in the communication chamber in case you needed to contact me, although I had a suspicion you'd turn up here sooner or later." Neethermire smiled broadly as he moved closer to Santa.

Santa didn't hesitate before wrapping Neethermire in a huge hug; he picked up the old elf as he squeezed him tight. "I can always count on you, my friend," he said, gently setting Neethermire down on his feet.

Noah couldn't help but interrupt. "Did you say there's a communication chamber up there?" he asked. "So, I wasn't going crazy when I heard that message last night?"

"Of course not," Santa said, his booming voice echoing throughout the vast water park. "When I realized I had been betrayed, I didn't have much time to put plans into motion, but I acted as quickly as I could. I used my power to create the storm that led you to the North Point Resort. You see, this place is in your realm, but we keep it shrouded with magic so that humans cannot accidentally stumble across it. I wasn't sure that it would work, but I took my chances. Then I sent that communication just as Malachi's minions came for me. Only the crystal's magic could have unlocked my message, so it's good to know you carry it everywhere." Santa directed a wink at Noah.

Noah felt completely starstruck that Santa Claus was paying attention to him. The way the big man looked at him made him feel all warm inside.

Meanwhile, Alex looked down at his shoes, feeling left out and jealous that Santa was only speaking to Noah. He didn't want to admit it, but he realized he had actually been feeling jealous ever since he had first seen Noah use his crystal. For a brief moment, he wondered if that was how Malachi had felt when he and Santa were boys.

As if sensing Alex's gloominess, Santa turned to Alex, and without warning, wrapped him in a huge bear hug. He chuckled deeply as he set the boy back down, "In case you haven't noticed, I'm a hugger," Santa said.

He then stooped down to look Alex directly in the eye. "Thank you for getting my crystal back. That was incredibly quick thinking on your part, not to mention very brave of you. While Malachi still has my powers, at least we stand a chance since he doesn't have the crystal to channel the magic through."

Santa then turned to Anna and Edward and hugged them each in turn, both parents giggling like children as Santa lifted them from their feet. "It seems I owe your entire family a great debt of gratitude. While I know this fight is far from over, I wouldn't be here without you."

A soft moan from the ground shifted everyone's attention to Athena, who lay on a bed of towels that Santa had placed her on as soon as they had come through the portal. Her eyes were still closed and her breathing was shallow, but she was still alive.

Santa moved immediately toward the fox. Kneeling next to her, he cradled Athena's head in his large hands. He spoke to her in a soft voice. "You made a great sacrifice for me, my true friend. I will never forget your courage." A tear ran down his face. "But I need you to keep fighting. Please don't give up." He then stroked her head and whispered something in her ear. Even though she was unconscious, a small smile passed her lips.

He then turned to Neethermire. "Is North Point secure?" Santa asked. "We need to get Athena to the medical bay immediately." Though he spoke with conviction, his eyes betrayed how worried he was about the white fox.

"And take the elves to see the doctor as well," Santa continued, gesturing toward Izzy's parents and the other elves that had been affected by the HAJE. "I'm not sure what we can do for them right now, but once we can get our hands on Malachi's weapon, hopefully we can find a cure for them."

"Yes, Sir," the ancient elf said, just as two elves arrived with a stretcher to carry Athena to the doctor. Izzy, her parents, and the other elves followed close behind. "Between the loyal elves and the nutcracker soldiers, we were able to drive the enemy out. I am ashamed to say that there were several traitorous elves who aided the goblins by opening portals to help them escape when they realized they could not defeat us."

"You should feel no shame," Santa Claus said. "This is not your fault. Malachi must have been plotting this for years, if not decades. I don't know what he has promised these elves, but it seems that he has turned many more to his side than I ever could have thought possible."

"Well, Sir, I actually do know what he has promised. While most of the traitors were able to flee with the goblins, we were able to apprehend one," Neethermire said hesitantly. "It turns out that some of the elves have ambitions beyond the North Pole. It seems that Malachi has promised them each control of their own territory once he has taken over the world. He persuaded them with tales of power and riches that I thought elves were immune to. I am deeply troubled to know that I was wrong."

"As am I," Santa replied sadly. "But there's no time to think about that now. We'll deal with those elves later. The most important thing right now is saving Christmas! We have to ensure that Christmas magic endures at all costs."

In that moment, a switch seemed to flip in Santa, turning him from the kindhearted, bear-hugging Santa to a capable leader who was ready to do whatever it took to protect what he loved most.

"I'm already on that," Neethermire said with a hint of pride. "I've made sure the backup plans have been put in motion. There's just one major detail standing in our way, and that's the fact that we can't exactly save Christmas while you don't have access to your powers. I mean, you can't even fly a sleigh without them, let alone cross dimensions to enter the world and deliver millions of gifts in one night."

Noah wondered how Neethermire knew about Santa losing his powers. No one had said anything about it, but before Noah could ask, Alex interrupted.

"Uh, we might have one more problem," Alex said. He then told the group about how he had seen Malachi escaping back at the command center.

Santa stroked his beard, looking troubled. "If Malachi was unharmed, he is no doubt reassembling his forces as we speak. If I know my brother, he will not wait to strike. We must ready ourselves!"

"Understood," Neethermire said. "I'll be back shortly." And with that, he quickly left the water park as if on a mission.

Noah and Alex looked to their parents, both boys afraid of what was to come. Anna and Edward hugged their children tightly. "What can we do, Santa? We want to help," Anna said. Edward nodded his head in agreement.

"The best way to help is by protecting these boys, which I know I don't need to instruct you to do. It's too much to explain now, but the North Pole's future rests on the shoulders of these two boys, the Sons of the Crystal," Santa said firmly. "I want you to hide until either Neethermire or I come to get you. Trust no one else, do you understand?"

The James family all nodded their heads, then headed toward the exit in search of a place to hide. They had almost reached the doors when something flung them open and in stepped Malachi, followed by a small army of goblins.

His dark clothes were torn and tattered and he was limping. His long white hair hung like curtains, hiding his face as he strode into the water park. As he came closer, it was clear that his face was badly bruised and cut in several places. While it was obvious that Malachi was injured, the look of determination and anger in his eyes made it clear that he would push through any pain.

"Leaving so soon?" Malachi said to the James family as they backed away from him and his hoard of goblins. "No, no, no, that won't do at all. The party is just getting started . . . and you boys are the guests of honor."

16

A WET WAR

"You will not touch a hair on their heads," a voice bellowed from behind Noah and Alex. They turned to see Santa Claus stalking toward his brother with a fearless determination in his eyes. His march was truly magnificent—his steps strong and sure, his large body ready for battle. His fierce demeanor seemed at odds with the traditional view of Santa Claus, but this jolly Saint Nick clearly had a warrior's spirit when provoked.

"And who exactly is going to stop me?" Malachi asked with an evil grin. "It seems you are all alone here except for that troublesome family. But not to worry, I'll deal with them soon enough. Right after I take care of you, brother."

In that moment, Malachi rushed toward his brother. Santa met him head-on, the two colliding explosively, then locking into battle. Santa Claus was the first to get in a blow as he stepped quickly toward his brother. In one smooth motion, Santa grabbed Malachi by the shoulders and swept his leg out from under him, sending Malachi crashing hard to the ground. He grunted in pain, but reacted quickly. He rolled away from Santa and scrambled back to his feet. It was clear he and Santa were both skilled fighters as they traded rapid strikes and kicks.

"Get the boys!" Malachi screamed at the goblins who seemed unsure what to do.

Before the goblins could react, Noah pulled the crystal from his pocket and held it above his head. It was glowing bright red. The goblins hesitated for a moment before slowly moving toward the family.

Noah aimed the crystal at one of the large icicles hanging from the ceiling. With laser-like precision, he used the crystal's red ray to sever a massive icicle hanging over the goblins. The bulk of the ice came crashing down, hitting several goblins head-on and scattering the rest. "I'm getting pretty good at this," Noah said as he aimed it at another icicle.

Paying more attention to the ceiling than what was going on around him, Noah didn't notice that a small group of goblins wielding a variety of weapons had managed to get very close to him and his family. The creatures were drawing around them slowly to form a circle.

Alex saw a large hole in the enemy's forces and ran through to the other side. "Noah!" he yelled. "Throw me the crystal!"

Without hesitating, Noah lobbed the crystal high, and it sailed over the goblins' heads. Alex caught it smoothly from the air and immediately released several blue blasts from the crystal's tip. The goblins who were struck were frozen instantly, while the others pushed and shoved each other to get away, some going as far as trying to use their companions as shields.

Having once again scattered the goblins, the James family ran. "Follow me," Alex said. "If we can put enough distance between us and them, we will have enough time to open a portal and get out of here."

The main doors were still blocked by thirty or more goblins, who didn't seem in a hurry to join the fight. Malachi, who was still locked in hand-to-hand combat with Santa Claus, roared, "After them, you fools!" A second later, Santa landed a heavy kick right into Malachi's stomach. The evil brother doubled over with pain, but still he fought on.

It was enough to get the goblins moving, but just as they started after the boys, the doors were thrown open. Two huge nutcracker soldiers along with a handful of warrior elves rushed into the fray. There weren't many of them, but they were clearly skilled fighters and just enough of a distraction for the James family to make a break for it.

Noah wondered briefly why Neethermire hadn't returned yet. Clearly, he had sent the nutcrackers and elves to aid Santa, but where was he? The thought of Neethermire reminded Noah of the hidden communication center inside the Avalanche waterslide. If he and his family could find it, they could maybe wait things out there. He told his family the idea, and they all agreed it was a good plan.

Once atop the hill of the Avalanche, the James family turned back and were shocked by what they saw. In only a few moments, the elf warriors and nutcrackers had managed to turn the tides and were now in complete control of the situation.

It was a hilarious sight. One of the nutcracker soldiers had driven a group of goblins deep into the wave pool. The creatures were too afraid to come out and face the nutcracker, so they stayed there, getting washed over with each passing surge of water. It was obvious the goblins could not swim, as they came up sputtering and gasping for air after each wave.

Other goblins had scattered and were trying to escape down waterslides. The creatures looked comical as they twisted and turned with their gangly arms and legs splayed out as they plunged down the slides. The more graceful elves chased closely behind, capturing the goblins the moment they landed in the pools.

Two of the elves were standing on inner tubes with their swords drawn, chasing goblins on rafts down the lazy river. The goblins tried to paddle faster to escape the elves, but the warriors overtook them in no time. With the fluid motion of trained swordsmen, the elves popped each of the rafts with a single stroke, leaving the goblins desperately trying to stay atop their rapidly deflating floats.

The strangest sight by far was Santa chasing Malachi down a waterslide on the other side of the park. Noah and Alex had watched as Malachi, realizing the tides were turning in Santa's favor, had tried to flee. He had taken off at a run and Santa had chased after him. Malachi ran hard, but soon found he had nowhere else to go but down a large open slide.

The family enjoyed the view immensely. Malachi slipped and rolled down the slide, his arms and feet flailing wildly.

Santa, however, was in complete control, yelling "Yippee!" as he followed Malachi down. While most of the waterslide was an open tube, the very bottom was an enclosed tunnel that ended with a slight ramp, which would spit the rider out high in the sky before they would splash down in a pool below.

While Santa knew the slide well, Malachi was unaware of the enclosure at the bottom of the slide. He had turned around to look at Santa, but turned back just in time to see the tunnel. For anyone of normal size, the tunnel would not have posed a problem, but the massive Malachi hit his head on the lip of the tunnel entrance, knocking him unconscious instantly. He was spit out the other end and flopped helplessly into the pool.

Santa, knowing what to expect, simply ducked his head and was shot into the air. He landed with a big splash next to his unconscious brother, who was floating face down in the pool. Alex, Noah, and their parents watched as Santa swam to Malachi and immediately turned him over. Malachi's heavy cloak was threatening to pull him underwater, but Santa was able to lift him from the pool with ease.

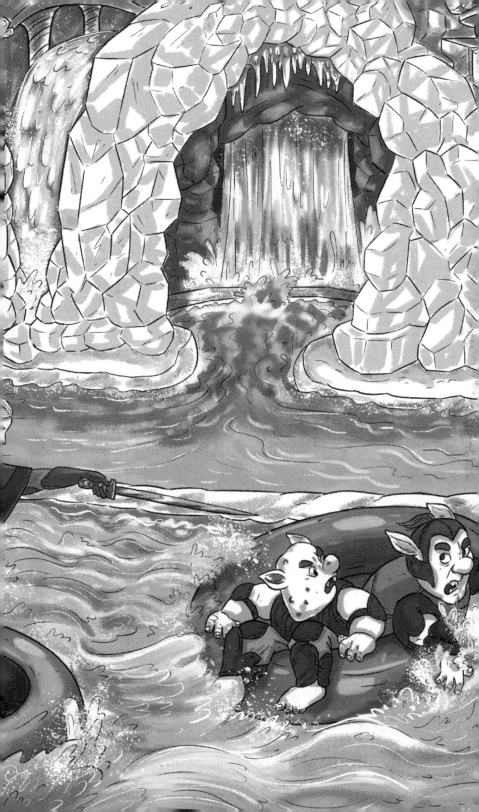

Santa looked down at his brother with concern until Malachi slowly opened his eyes, lifted his head slightly, and said, in a voice that sounded like a growl, "This isn't over." But before he could say anything more, his eyes closed and his head fell back to the concrete.

"Get him out of here!" Santa commanded two nearby elves. "Lock him in the cellars until we can get him back to the North Pole. And take the rest of them with you," he instructed, indicating the goblins who had given up all fight even before Malachi had been defeated.

Seeing that the situation was well under control, the James family decided to head back down to join Santa. The boys started to walk down the hill, but Anna stopped them. "No reason everyone else should have all the fun," she said with a wink. "Last one down is a rotten egg!" Then she jumped into the mouth of the Avalanche. Edward and the boys were close behind her, all fully clothed, speeding down the waterslide.

When they splashed down in the pool below, Alex swam over to his brother. "Here, I bet you want this back," Alex said, holding the crystal out to Noah.

"That's OK," Noah said. "Why don't you hold on to it for a while? It looks like it's not just my lucky crystal anymore. And honestly, I'm happy to share it with you. The last thing I want is to wind up like Santa and Malachi. Whatever happens in the future, we're going to do it together."

"Yeah, together," Alex agreed with a smile.

Their parents, who were nearby, heard the whole thing and smiled at each other, thinking how sweet their boys could be. That was, until Alex grabbed Noah by the head and dunked him underwater. Noah came up laughing and splashing his brother back.

When the family emerged from the pool, Santa was waiting for them. "I'm starving," the big man said with a grin. "Who wants some pizza?"

"Now you're talking," Alex said, heading toward the door.

They were almost out the door when a portal opened nearby, and out poured a small army of animals with Neethermire at the front. It was the group of animals that had gathered at Eveline's and included mice, rabbits, wolves, polar bears, and owls.

Toward the back of the procession, Noah and Alex spotted Eveline walking quickly toward them. They ran to her and hugged her, thankful that she was OK. Santa was right behind them, picking up his mother with great love as he wrapped her in one of his bear hugs.

145

Eveline cupped Santa's face in her hands. "Thank goodness you're OK," she said with a soft sigh. "And your brother?" she asked, hopeful that Malachi was not harmed. While she could not tolerate what her son had done, he was her child and she would love him always.

"He's fine, Mom," Santa said. "He's just going to wake up with a pretty huge headache." Noah could see Santa was trying to hold back a smile.

"What a shame, it appears we are too late and have missed all the action," Neethermire said as he joined Santa. "I thought Malachi would have put up more of a fight."

"You're not late at all." Santa laughed. "We had it handled, didn't we, boys?" he said to Noah and Alex.

Then he turned back to Neethermire. "I'm glad you brought reinforcements. We're going to need all the help we can get if we're going to save Christmas. But first, pizza!"

A PLAN FOR CHRISTMAS

The group sat around the fireplace in the restaurant, enjoying the most delicious pizza that Alex and Noah had ever tasted. After the day they'd had, everyone was exhausted and ready for a break, but as soon as they were done eating, Santa announced that there was lots of work to do . . . in the morning. Then he sent everyone off to get a good night's sleep while he and Neethermire tended to Malachi and his minions.

The James family made their way back to the room and fell into bed. Anna and Edward dozed off right away, while the boys, who were still too excited from the day's events, stayed up whispering about all that had happened.

"Can you believe that half-pipe today? It was sick!" Alex said.

"Really?" Noah questioned, laughing quietly. "We traveled to the North Pole today, saw a bunch of talking animals, rescued our parents from a madman, met and saved Santa Claus, and you are talking about snowboarding? Priorities, man!" Noah tossed a pillow at his brother.

"OK, fine," Alex said. "What about that part where it sounded like one of us is going to be the next Santa Claus? How's that for an important part of the day?"

"We don't know that for sure," Noah said, "but like we talked about earlier, no matter what happens, we stick together, right?"

"Absolutely, little bro," Alex said with a big yawn, then drifted off to sleep.

Sleep came a bit more slowly to Noah, who lay awake thinking about the idea of either he or Alex being Santa one day. While they had promised to always have each other's backs, would things change some day like they had for Santa and Malachi? He pushed the thought from his mind and finally fell asleep.

The next morning, the boys woke when Anna threw back the curtains, letting blazing sunlight into the room. "C'mon Mom, just a little bit longer," Alex groaned, burying his head under the pillow.

"Not a chance," she said excitedly. "In case you forgot, we get to help save Christmas, and I for one am not missing out on this once-in-a-lifetime opportunity."

The family made their way downstairs and found that everyone was already assembled by the enormous fireplace in the lobby. Santa and Neethermire sat by the fire, facing a group of elves and animals alike.

"Good morning, James family," Santa said cheerfully. "Hot cocoa?" He gestured at two nearby elves to bring the warm drinks. Noah's mouth was already watering as he thanked the elf, then took the steaming cup of creamy cocoa.

"Allow me to introduce you all to the members of the emergency council," Santa said. He then went on to explain that each of the elves on the council represented one of the six guilds that made up the North Pole's Christmas operations. The guilds were for toy makers, gift packagers, book writers, holiday bakers, and musicians. There was also a Christmas cheer guild. The animals on the council each represented one of the creature clans of the North Pole's forests.

Towering above the group sat Arnan. The boys' hearts warmed as Arnan looked at them and smiled. They hadn't seen him since they left him back at the workshop, and they were very relieved to see he was all right.

"OK, now that everyone knows each other, we can get started," Santa announced. "We have less than four full days to pull off Christmas this year, and we face more obstacles than we ever have before.

"First of all, the North Pole is in shambles. During Malachi's brief time in charge, he managed to halt operations long enough that we now have very few supplies there. I currently have elves in the Pole collecting any toys or items they can find, but the plan is to use North Point as our operations base. With that said, Christmas is going to look very different this year."

"Excuse me, Sir, but what exactly do you mean by different?" the elf who was the head of the toy makers guild asked, looking concerned. "My elves and I can't possibly make the number of toys needed by Christmas Eve."

"I'll get to that in a moment," Santa said. "The second, and probably most important, issue is that I no longer have my powers." A collective gasp rose from the elves and animals as they all looked around at each other, obviously worried.

"I transferred my powers to Malachi," Santa continued. "I have the crystal, but I cannot wield its power unless

Malachi willingly gives the power back. I don't see that happening, but that is a problem for later. I do not regret my decision, as I did what I had to do in the moment, but this poses our greatest challenge. A challenge that I hope I have a solution for. Boys, I trust you have your crystal with you?"

"Yes, Sir," Noah and Alex answered in unison. Then Noah said shyly, "But I'm not sure how our crystal can help. The only thing we've been able to make it do is melt things and freeze them. I can't see how that will be very useful in saving Christmas."

"Don't forget about opening portals," Alex chimed in.

"Oh, dear boys, that is just the tip of the iceberg of what your crystal can do," Santa said. "It will take years of training for you to fully understand its powers, but for now we will stick with the basics, and hopefully it will be enough to make sure the world still has a great Christmas."

Noah and Alex looked at each other, exchanging uneasy glances. "Years of training? What have we gotten ourselves into?" Noah whispered.

"OK, back to our first problem," Santa said. "If you'll all follow me, I have something to show you."

The entire group followed Santa as he walked outside into the icy morning. He led them to the first chairlift, but rather than getting on the lift, Santa stepped into the control booth. He pushed a few buttons inside, then put his face against a panel on the wall, where a small laser scanned his eye.

"Access granted. Welcome, Santa," a computerized voice said. Outside the booth, the ground beneath the boys began to shake. Noah's first thought was an avalanche, but when he looked at the mountain, he saw that the rumbling was the result of a huge secret door that was sliding open on the mountainside. The entrance led to an immense cavern that was carved deep into the mountain. They all followed Santa inside.

"Oh yes, this will do. This will do," the head elf of the toy makers guild said with surprise as they entered the cave and saw it was completely filled with toys and games. As the boys looked closer, they realized that while all the gifts looked brand new, they appeared to be very old-fashioned.

There were no video games or electronics; there were really no modern toys at all. Alex and Noah wandered through the great cave, touching and playing with things as they went. They saw puzzles and toys carved from wood. They saw antique bicycles, unicycles, and even some bikes built for two. There were roller skates and hand-carved rocking horses. There were dolls made from porcelain, dolls made from cloth, and even dolls made from paper.

The outer walls of the cave were stacked with beautifully bound books that smelled richly of old paper and ink. There was also an abundance of board games; some had names the boys recognized, even if the packaging looked very different. Anna picked up an original version of Candyland and showed it to the boys.

"Ah yes," a voice interrupted. Santa had come up behind them. "That game first came out in 1949. I remember it well, as it was the year I took over from the previous Santa Claus. It was a bit of a rough start for me that year, as I completely went overboard on my numbers. The elves thought I was crazy to request so many toys be made that year. Turns out they were right and we had quite a lot of extra toys."

"Wow, so all of this was left over from one Christmas?" Alex asked.

Santa smiled. "Well, not exactly," he said. "I was a bit of a slow learner, and I didn't take advice well back then. It took me several years to get the hang of things, and by that point all of these extra treasures had accumulated. We have kept them here for an emergency such as this. These gifts are not what children will be expecting this Christmas, but I know they will bring joy."

The boys continued to walk through the vast cavern as Anna and Edward stopped to look at more old board games, books, and toys.

Santa caught up with the boys after a few minutes. He put an arm around each of the brothers and said, "Alright boys, now that everyone knows their jobs, it's time for us to get to work."

THE BIG SHOW

The next few days were a whirlwind of activity at the North Point Ski Resort. The James brothers spent most of their time training with Santa while their parents aided the elves and animals in preparing for Christmas.

The first order of business had been perfecting the boys' portal-opening ability. Without Santa's powers, he would need the boys to help him get quickly from place to place on Christmas Eve. The boys had been absolutely thrilled when they learned that they were going to ride with Santa in order to open the portals for him.

The next thing they practiced was the ability to make the reindeer and sleigh fly. Alex mastered this skill quickly, while Noah struggled a bit more to get it, but after day two, both boys were more than capable of the task.

They worked long and hard, and by the morning of Christmas Eve, Santa told them they were ready for the big show. "Now, go take a well-deserved break while I check my lists twice," Santa said with a wink. The boys didn't hesitate before heading out to find some hot chocolate.

"I can't believe we are actually going to do this," Alex said, with such excitement that he was bouncing.

"I know," Noah said, but he wasn't as excited as his brother. The truth was that Noah was worried about messing things up. He sometimes wished he was more carefree like his brother, but in that moment, he felt the weight of the world's happiness on his shoulders.

A few seconds later, the boys bumped into their parents on the way to the restaurant. It felt like they hadn't seen each other much at all over the past couple of days. Anna and Edward could both sense that Noah was troubled. "Hey guys," Anna said cheerily as she hugged each of her sons. "It looks like your father and I have done all we can do for now. What do you say we all hit the slopes for a bit?"

Both Noah and Alex thought that sounded like a great idea, and within fifteen minutes they were all riding up the chairlift together. About midway up the mountain, Edward told the boys he had a surprise for them. "It seems that Santa's sleigh actually has enough seating for five," Edward said enthusiastically. "And he's invited us to come along tonight."

Noah's heart lifted at the idea that his parents would be with them. Just the knowledge that he would have them nearby made him feel instantly braver.

Alex, Noah, and their parents spent the next couple of hours enjoying the crisp mountain air and empty mountain. The boys had no idea what adventures lay in store for them, but in those moments, all they focused on was having fun with their family.

Later that night, when all the final details had been attended to and the last gift had been strapped down, the James family climbed aboard the sleigh. Anna and Edward settled in the back. They held warm thermoses of hot cocoa while they covered themselves in fur blankets, snuggling against each other and enjoying the sheer magic of the evening. Santa motioned for the boys to sit next to him on the front bench of the sleigh.

Santa then stood briefly and thanked everyone who had gathered to see them off. "Because of all your hard work, we were able to save Christmas," Santa said, his voice echoing off the surrounding mountains. "We will have a true celebration when we return, but for now I'd just like to say Merry Christmas to all, and to all a good night." The elves and animals cheered loudly as Santa sat back down.

"Alright boys," Santa said to Alex and Noah, "which of you would like to do the honors of making us fly?"

The brothers looked at each other, then Noah said, "I think we'd like to do it together."

Alex flashed a huge smile.

"A perfect idea," Santa said.

Alex and Noah stood slightly, each placing a hand on the crystal, grasping it tightly. Each raised his arm so that the crystal formed a brightly glowing point between them. They focused their thoughts as they recalled their training. Within seconds the sleigh was airborne, and they hovered for just a moment, waving at those below. Alex caught sight of Izzy just as they were about to get going. She was standing with Neethermire and Eveline, and she looked happy as she smiled up at them.

"OK, it's time," Santa said. "Open the first portal." The boys did as they were instructed, and in seconds they had vanished into the dark night sky.

The children of the world were indeed surprised when they woke on Christmas morning to find old-fashioned toys under their trees rather than the things they had put on their lists. At first, there was some disappointment. However, before long children were discovering the delight in such simple books, toys, and games. Entire families read and played together, the kids experiencing something different while older generations reveled in the nostalgia of the gifts.

Many families labeled it the best Christmas ever as joy and laughter filled their homes.

Back at the North Point Ski Resort, a true feast had been laid out after Santa and the James family had taken some time to rest from the extremely long night they had just had. Alex and Noah came down to the great lobby to see twenty long wooden tables that were filled with every kind of holiday food they could hope for. Starving, since they hadn't eaten much all night, the boys couldn't wait to try all the delicious food on display.

"Dig in, boys," Santa said, coming to stand beside them. "You two deserve it."

Anna and Edward joined the boys and Santa as they sat down to an amazing Christmas meal. The boys piled their plates high with mostly desserts until they saw Anna watching them, then they added a bit of "real food" just to make her happy.

When they had eaten until they couldn't take another bite, Santa asked them to follow him over to the enormous Christmas tree, where brightly wrapped packages were piled high beneath its branches. He went straight for two boxes that had Alex's and Noah's names on them.

The boys unwrapped the presents, Alex tearing off the wrapping paper while Noah took his time. Inside the boxes were two identical snow globes, each one showing Santa standing alone in the center with no other detail inside—no trees, no snow, no workshop.

"These are so you can find me any time you need me," Santa Claus said. "Just use your crystal and focus on the globe, and no matter where I am, even in another realm, it will bring you straight to me. However, you should only use this power in case of emergency."

"So, we're not going with you back to the North Pole," Alex asked, sounding disappointed.

"Not yet, boys. Had it not been for Malachi's rebellion, I would not have sent for you two for several more years. One day, I will bring you back with me, but now is not the time."

Noah was secretly relieved to hear that they would be headed home instead of on any more quests at the moment.

The next day, the James family said goodbye to everyone, then packed their car and headed home. "What a wild adventure, huh boys," Edward said as they drove away. "Somehow I think next year's vacation won't quite live up to the excitement of this year . . . but we can always try." He laughed.

Noah turned back to get one more glance at the North Point Ski Resort as they drove out of the parking lot. His breath caught when all he saw was a wide-open field where the beautiful building had just stood. He looked all over in disbelief, but the entire place had truly just disappeared.

Before he could say anything, Noah looked down and saw his backpack glowing brightly. He reached inside and pulled out the crystal. Alex was now paying attention as well, and the two watched as the crystal pulsed dazzlingly three times . . . then the light went out. Both boys tried their best to use the crystal's powers, but it was no use. The crystal had gone back to sleep.

EPILOGUE

Eleven Months Later

It was Thanksgiving Day in the North Pole, and operations were back to normal after the turmoil of the previous year . . . well, almost back to normal. Santa was just returning from a Christmas practice run on a new sleigh that did not require magic to fly.

"How'd it go?" asked an eager young elf named Jorn, who had developed the technology that ran the new sleigh.

"It went splendidly. And truth be told, I think the reindeer will probably enjoy having the night off this year," Santa said cheerfully, even though he was completely drained of energy. "I still can't access Christmas magic, but between Neethermire opening the existing portals for me and the new sleigh, it seems like we've found a good solution to delivering Christmas until Malachi transfers my powers back to me."

Jorn beamed at Santa's compliment as he went to work checking the sleigh over. "Speaking of your brother, Sir," the young elf said as Santa started to walk away, "your mother has asked that you find her before you visit him this evening."

Santa nodded and headed out to find his mom. He had been visiting his brother in the dungeon every day since Malachi had been captured. While Malachi had yet to speak to Santa, Santa held hope that one day, things would be different.

As he walked through the village, Santa was reminded that the North Pole was still dark and gloomy as a result of Malachi's rebellion. Santa could not put things back the way they had been because he was unable to touch Christmas magic. The elves had still been able to do their jobs, but the shadow that hung over the North Pole made everything seem cheerless.

Santa sighed as he reminded himself that the most important part of Christmas magic was not his to control. As long as there was enough magic stored in the North Pole, it would automatically be released into the world around Christmas time. They had barely succeeded last Christmas in making sure the magic had been refilled. He was hopeful they would be able to pull it off again this year. Even if things didn't look quite as they had, Santa would continue to push on, until either Malachi gave back his power . . . or a new Santa was chosen.

Santa was pulled from his thoughts as he finally reached the lodge. "Good afternoon," Eveline said with a huge smile as Santa entered. He picked her up and swung her around, then set her gently back down.

"So, I know you must be absolutely exhausted," Eveline started, "but I was wondering if we could maybe go visit your brother together today before you go to rest? It's just that it is Thanksgiving, and while I know he's where he needs to be, it still breaks my heart to think of him alone down there."

Santa fought the urge to say that Malachi wasn't alone down there because he had all his goblin friends with him, but instead he just nodded and said, "Sure mom, we can go visit him now. I had planned to bring him Thanksgiving dinner a bit later, but we can stop to pick up his favorites on the way."

Eveline felt hopeful as she and Santa descended the stairs to the cells. It was much brighter down there now that there were full-time captives in the prison. Santa had tried to provide as much comfort for his brother as possible, and even though Malachi wouldn't admit it, Santa knew that his brother enjoyed the little luxuries, especially the food and books.

As they got closer to Malachi's cell, Santa was thinking of what else his brother might enjoy to make being locked up more tolerable. "If only he would transfer back my powers, I could let him go," Santa thought to himself. He truly hated having to keep his brother prisoner, but he was also keenly aware of what would happen if he did not.

All those thoughts were pushed aside as Santa and Eveline rounded the corner to see the door of Malachi's cell wide open. Adrenaline replaced Santa's exhaustion as he ran to the gate. He looked inside the cell, his fears confirmed. Malachi was gone!

Did you like Magic in the Mountains?

Your opinion matters!

Thank you so much for reading *Magic in the Mountains*. Online reviews are very important for authors like me as they help readers discover new books. If you enjoyed this book, I would love to see your review on **Amazon** or **Goodreads**. Your reviews really do make a difference.

Happy reading,

T.E. Milburn

ABOUT THE AUTHOR

T.E. Milburn dreamed of being an author since she was a little girl. In the third grade, T.E. Milburn won first prize in a creative story writing contest. Having realized her dream, she then decided to take a break from writing for the next thirty-five years.

Until one day, T.E. Milburn was yanked back into the writing world while helping her sons with a homeschool assignment. What started as a fun family project turned into the novel you have in your hands. T.E. Milburn truly hopes you enjoy this holiday tale that has combined her love of adventure, magic, and Christmas.

Made in the USA
Monee, IL
01 November 2023